THE FUTURE
IS YOURS

THE FUTURE IS YOURS

Introducing Future Life Progression –
the dynamic technique that reveals
your destiny

ANNE JIRSCH
AND
MONICA CAFFERKY

piatkus

PIATKUS

First published in Great Britain in 2007 by Piatkus Books
This edition published in 2011 by Piatkus

A CIP catalogue record for this book
is available from the British Library.

ISBN 978-0-7499-3984-7

Text design by Briony Chappell
Edited by Liz Dean

Data manipulation by
Action Publishing Technology Ltd, Gloucester
Printed and bound in Great Britain by
CPI Mackays

Piatkus
An imprint of
Little, Brown Book Group
100 Victoria Embankment
London EC4Y 0DY

An Hachette UK Company

www.piatkus.co.uk

Contents

Acknowledgements

I would like to thank:

Paul McKenna for your wisdom, support and kindness.

Dave Brown for your dedication from day one and for your incredibly accurate predictions.

Steve Goldie for your support and insights throughout the journey.

And Monica Cafferky for her dedication and belief in my work.

Also, the following people need a special thank you for permissions granted to quote from their work or for giving time for interviews: Dr Oliver Curry, from the Darwin Research Centre at the London School of Economics; Sara Davidson; Chris Ellis; Dr Bruce Goldberg, a true pioneer and author of *Egypt: An Extraterrestrial And Time Traveler Experiment* and *Time Travelers from Our Future;* Greg Secker; and the many wonderful people who have taken part in my Future Life Progression workshops and studies.

Anne Jirsch

Foreword
by Paul McKenna

People often ask me, 'What is future life progression?' and I say the simplest answer is that it's like seeing a snapshot of your karma. But really, the simple answer is that there isn't a simple answer! However, is the process of value? I believe the answer is definitely yes!

Many corporations these days do something called 'strategic planning'. This is where executives sit (often with eyes closed) and imagine what products or services their company will be offering in the future and what their competitors will also be doing. That way they can benefit from hindsight ahead of time.

And so it is with any kind of future progression process. Your mind is the world's most advanced bio-computer and to ask it to calculate where you are going to end up, given where you are now, is a straightforward equation for it to do. However, because the future is not fixed it will almost certainly present you with several scenarios of what might happen.

Years ago, I did a visualisation process where I asked my mind to show me where I would be if I continued along the path I was on. At the time I was working as a radio broadcaster and so I saw myself older, more paranoid and certainly not spiritually or financially richer. So I asked my mind a different question, 'What would I do if I knew I couldn't fail?' and I saw myself working as a hypnotist on television, making self-improvement products and travelling around the world with a glamorous life. The process of imagining the future had shown me I had choices at any moment in time.

It's the same with Future Life Progression. Of course I am not suggesting we are actually physically travelling to the future, because it hasn't happened yet, but through a simple psychological process we can glimpse the possible futures which may await us.

I have myself, and indeed I know of many people who have done this process with Anne, and whether or not they believe the possible futures they have seen are real isn't important. Everyone benefits – and the experience can be very entertaining, but more often immensely enlightening.

After working with people in the area of personal change for the last 20 years, I am convinced that if everyone took a little time to really consider their future, they would be a lot happier.

It is because Anne has spent years researching this area that she has been able to write this wonderful book, which contains within it the tools to glimpse your future, so that you can create the one you want.

Paul McKenna

THE FUTURE
IS YOURS

For my wonderful daughters, Zoe and Lucy

CHAPTER 1

Working with Future Life Progression

Imagine being able to travel into the future and see what will be happening in your life, and in the world and beyond. Imagine seeing who is in your life, where you work and live. What would it be like to have the ability to see which decisions will work out in your favour – and which will turn out to be disasters? How would you feel if you could jump into the future, right now, to discover the solutions to your present problems?

We have all, at some point, wished we had the benefit of hindsight or have thought, 'If only I knew then what I know now.' Just imagine if you could travel back in time right now and have a word with yourself. What advice would you impart? No doubt you would give clear information on who to have in your life and whom to avoid, what career moves to make and how to develop your talents. I bet you would even have something to say about who to marry, or live with, and where to buy a house.

I have taken jumps forward in time, and I have seen into the future. Some jumps were short, maybe three months, while others have spanned many years and even lifetimes. What I have witnessed is more amazing than any science-fiction movie. I haven't been using some special space ship. I have been time-travelling with my mind using a process called Future Life Progression, or FLP.

How does Future Life Progression work?

FLP works on the same basis as Past Life Regression (PLR) but instead of moving into the past, you jump into the future. Using the powerful visualization techniques described in the following chapters, you will soon have the ability to travel through time and explore the years ahead. This may sound unbelievable, but trust me – FLP is quick and simple to master, and this method really does work. I use it every day with my clients, who range from housewives to Hollywood film directors. I have been using this remarkable technique for six years, and it has changed my life. I know what I need to do, who I need to have around me and I have identified my soul's purpose – the spiritual reason I chose to have this particular life. Even more amazingly, the things I have seen many years into the future have often happened much sooner, and in some cases within days. By seeing the future I have brought it towards me and speeded up time from the future to the present. I have also spoken to my future self and gained insight and advice – hindsight. I hope to give you the tools to do the same.

How Future Life Progression will change your life

With tarot, or any form of fortune telling, the subject sits and listens to the reader or clairvoyant, who then relays their impressions to the subject. But FLP is different. With FLP you will live it for yourself, sometimes in full Technicolor! On some level, you will experience your own future for yourself rather than just being told someone else's predictions of your future. As one client put it, 'I could actually feel the heat of the sun in my future holiday. It was so real that I know it will happen.' You will have this experience too and my aim is that by reading this book and following the techniques, you will use FLP to improve every area of your life. By following the exercises you will be able to make the right choices and decisions with dilemmas concerning love, work, finances and even your soul's purpose.

In *The Future Is Yours*:

◆ You will learn how to use FLP to find 'the one' – your soul mate

◆ You will learn how to discover your inner genius to write that novel, play, song or script

◆ You will acquire quick and easy FLP techniques to make sparkling decisions at work

◆ You will look ahead at economic trends to help you to benefit from your investments, identify property 'hot spots' and avoid investing in markets or products that will become obsolete

◆ You will examine your past, present and future to find any reoccurring issues or problems that have plagued you throughout time and enable you to clear them immediately

◆ You will connect with your soul and realise just how wonderful you truly are as you find your own true essence, your soul's purpose

◆ You will look at yourself in your next lifetime to find out how you evolve. You will even be able to talk to your future self and tap into your future wisdom. If you wish, you could even glimpse the future of humankind. In fact, there's not an area of your life in which FLP can't benefit you in some way

Does this sound fantastic – almost too good to be true? I am sure it does, yet when you travel into the future with Future Life Progression you will find answers to many of the vital questions you have right now. I have taken many of my clients forward in time and it has changed their lives. I am about to show you exactly what to do to change yours.

How my journey to the future began

Since I was a child I have been fascinated with seeing in to the future. My grandmother Winny, who was originally from London's East End, was my inspiration for wanting to be psychic. Gran read the tea leaves and had a constant stream of visitors to her house in Orpington, Kent, seeking her advice and wisdom. Every year I escaped from Notting Hill's poor back streets, in West London, to spend wonderful summers with her, watching and wishing I was like her. I wanted to be psychic so much it ached.

At 18 I packed my rucksack and headed East with £100 in my pocket, travelling from Istanbul to Kabul in Afghanistan. By the time I reached India I was searching for answers, and it was in the colourful and bustling city of Calcutta that my mind began to open to a new way of seeing the world. India awoke something in me and I felt my intuition bloom. I also met my first real mentor, after my grandmother, in the shape of a beggar named Vikram, who taught me how to let go and allow my psychic mind to flow.

In 1972 gap years were not the norm, and were especially unheard of for working-class girls like me. By then, most of my school friends were working in local factories or if they were lucky a shop. But me, I wanted to learn about the world, people and how to see the future. My quest, and my growing psychic awareness, led me to develop instant techniques for the mind and spirit which, collected together with my life story and real life case studies, were to form the basis of my first book, *Instant Intuition*.

After working as a psychic for most of my adult life, I experienced Future Life Progression long after I mastered many methods of fortune-telling, such as palmistry, tarot, astrology, runes and the I Ching. I've found all of these methods to be incredibly reliable – I have worked as a tarot consultant for nearly 30 years, and I find the cards continue to give astonishingly accurate predictions. I have also spent 20 years helping clients with Past Life Regression techniques. Yet when I came across Future Life Progression I knew that I had stepped into a new dimension; a dimension which would not only answer my many questions, but would also help me to evolve and even show me what I would have to do to make my heart's desires a reality.

The vast majority of events that have played a major part in my life have come from a series of coincidences. I have long since learnt to listen and know that when synchronicity is occurring I take note. So when Future Life Progression appeared in my life it seemed like a natural progression. A way of accessing information that was clearer, deeper and wiser. The difference between FLP and other methods of divination is that with this process you experience your own future directly, rather than having someone else read something for you, interpret the information and pass it on to you. The experience is incredibly powerful, dynamic and leaves a changing energy which fills you with vitality and a certainty about which direction to take. Now I know a tarot reading can be pretty good, but you can't beat eating the cake rather than just looking at it.

Jumping around in time: the first FLP session

The first time I came across FLP was during a session of Past Life Regression, in which you use hypnosis to access a deep part of someone's subconscious mind.

Think of the mind as a filing system. The subconscious mind is a drawer that you can't open yourself while you are awake. However, everything you feel and think is stored somewhere deep in that one drawer, which is like Doctor Who's tardis – huge and ever-expanding! The information stored in the drawer impacts upon your behaviour and can filter into your conscious waking mind. For example, at three years old you may be frightened by a dog and store the negative experience in your subconscious. At 14 you have a fear of dogs but have no idea why you are scared of these animals. It is because that experience is stored in the subconscious and is still filtering through to your conscious whenever you meet one of our furry friends – or think about them.

Psychologists, psychiatrists and indeed anyone who works with the mind are aware of the power of the subconscious in creating our thoughts and affecting how we think, feel and act. Many therapists who work in a spiritual way think that the subconscious mind not only stores experiences from this life, but also from previous existences. They know that the subconscious acts as a bridge between this reality and the 'super-conscious' – an even deeper part of your brain that I believe is linked with your higher self and the universe. Past life regression taps into the higher self, and this was particularly apparent in the session during which I first stumbled across Future Life Progression 13 years ago.

A young woman, Fiona, had come to me for a second Past Life Regression session. In her first session she had described life as a milkmaid in Austria. She was carefree, happy and lived to an old age. It had been a positive experience and when I asked her what she needed to learn from this lifetime she said, 'to enjoy peace.'

For some reason, I had the feeling of unfinished business and suggested that Fiona had another PLR session when she was ready. During this second session – which I can now see was a pivotal point in my own life – Fiona jumped forward in time.

At first, the session began as normal, as Fiona began to see her past-life experiences. She described life as a young man fighting in the trenches during World War One. She became distressed, so I quickly asked her to find another life she needed to talk about. Fiona replied, 'I am in uniform.' I presumed she would say she was once again a soldier but I'm always careful not to prompt clients, so I asked, 'What are your surroundings?' She responded, 'I am aboard a spacecraft and I am the captain.'

I admit that I thought this was all just her imagination, but then I began to have flashes of a space craft. Often during Past Life Regression I see images – snap shots of what my client is experiencing. This time I could see a space craft too, so I asked her what year it was. She answered, '2050'.

I decided to end the session. I was confused. I had just had my first experience of FLP, and I didn't know it.

I will be honest – seven years passed and I forgot about my experience with Fiona until I had another encounter six years ago, which was more dramatic, direct and one that I couldn't forget or ignore. This time I recognised what was happening, and the experience led me to finding my life's work.

Meeting the soldiers: fate steps into my life

My practice in Bray is near Windsor, Berkshire, and over time I've built up a client base from those in military service at the castle and barracks. The first time a soldier came to see me I was surprised as I imagined that military men would be cynical about my work. Anyway, as usual word got round about me and a steady stream of soldiers started to come for Tarot readings – and most of them wanted to know about their love lives! However, two of the army men, Dave and Steve, were intrigued not about romance but about their past lives. They both booked a Past Life Regression session one day apart. Little did any of us know just how much these sessions would change our lives.

Steve's regression

Steve's session proved to be one of the most dramatic I have ever seen in the 20 years I've been working with Past Life Regression. Steve began to describe sand dunes and searing heat, and he saw a type of tent with a canopy. He then heard exotic music and realised he was somewhere in Arabia. There was fascination in his voice as he told me he had never seen anything like this in his life as he watched an Arab girl dance. I asked him where he was from and what he was doing there and he replied, 'The crusades. I am a white male.'

After the session Steve recalled, 'I had a glimpse of another life aboard a big ship. We were Vikings. Dave was there too; this time we were fighting side by side. Then I glimpsed another where Dave and I were Red Indian braves. In that lifetime we were brothers, again fighting side by side.'

The regression had opened a floodgate of past life memories. We discussed his experiences, then I suggested, 'It may be an idea not to tell Dave what you have seen as it could influence his session tomorrow.' Steve agreed.

Dave's regression

In Dave's regression, I was half expecting him to go straight into a warrior situation, just as Steve had in his session. Instead, he told me how he was a little boy in wartime London. He described living in the East End by a railway station, and that he enjoyed his life and didn't worry one jot about the bombs. I then took him forward to his adulthood where he described life as a scrap metal merchant. Then Dave suddenly jolted, 'I can see a wolf, he is playful. We grew up together. He is my friend.'

'Who are you?' I asked.

'I am Apache.' Dave had jumped straight into another lifetime. I wasn't surprised, as this happens to clients occasionally. He recounted his life as an Indian brave, fighting side by side with Steve.

Steve and Dave recognised each other in their regression. It now made sense to them why they had encountered so many coincidences in their current lives, often finding themselves working in the same place and for the same people – high-profile clients or in war zones such as Iraq, protecting journalists as they travel from one place to another. Their paths seem determined to cross, and not just in their past lifetimes but again and again in their current lifetimes.

After their regressions, Steve and Dave became men with a mission, deciding to find out all they could about their past lives; they both had a natural ability for regression, and I gave them lessons. The pair then spent long nights working in security at home in the UK, when nothing much happened, regressing each other and discovering more and more.

Dave called me with an update. 'Hey Anne,' he began, 'we've both seen you in one of our past lives – but I don't want to tell you about it. You need to see it for yourself.' I agreed it was best that I hadn't been primed beforehand. If I saw the very same thing it would be mind-boggling.

Steve regressed me and I saw myself sitting cross-legged outside a tepee mixing herbs. It was a beautiful place of pure peace. Suddenly came the thunder of hooves as a rival tribe charged through our village. I felt a blow to my head – I actually felt my skull dent and cave in. I flinched and put my hands to my head and cried, 'I've been hit!' Strangely enough, I survived the attack and lived to tell the tale in the village, albeit with a big dent in my head.

Steve and Dave then related how they had both seen themselves charging through a village side by side, where one of them threw a tomahawk at my head. (I never found out which one of them it was, and they refused to tell me!)

After these regressions, it was obvious to me that we three had been destined to meet in our current life times – although none of us knew why. Steve insisted, 'Anne, you must know what this is all about.' He looked disappointed when I replied that I had no idea. But I felt that one thing was for sure: we would find out soon enough. I told Steve that things would begin to unfold very soon.

My instincts told me we needed to access our past lives to find the clues. We needed the missing pieces of the jigsaw and I was convinced that our past lives held the answer – so I suggested a Past Life Regression for us as a group. At that point I had no idea just how interesting things were about to get.

The Twin Towers progression: the future changes forever

We held the session in the boardroom of my offices, a stark room with bare white walls and a large shiny wooden table. The room was ideal because there were no distractions. It's sound-proof too, which allowed us to forget about the outside world and focus entirely on our session.

I brought in Dan, a student of mine, to lead us back in time. Dan had a knack with Past Life Regression and I knew I could trust him to guide us through the process. We dimmed the lights and fell silent as Dan spoke softly and used the techniques I had taught him to guide us to float back in time.

After taking us through relaxation techniques, Dan told us, 'Feel yourself floating back through time. Float all the way back to a previous life, one where you have all met before.'

All three of us sat in silence, our eyes closed. Eventually Dan asked, 'Steve, what are you aware of?'

'This is odd,' he replied, 'I don't know what is going on. All I can see are two skyscrapers next to each other. There is smoke coming out of them.' He paused. 'I don't know what all this means – I haven't gone back to a past life at all. Maybe my mind isn't right for this at the moment. I just can't see anything other than these skyscrapers.'

Dan said, 'Tell me what else you see.'

Steve continued. 'There's smoke coming out of the skyscrapers. I don't know where this is. There are people on the ground running, there is lots of dust. A helicopter is circling the building.' He added, 'It is not army, nor police. It says CNN. This is America.'

Dave then reported, 'I'm not seeing a past life either, but I'm not seeing what Steve is seeing. All I can see is a bay, but I don't recognise it. This sounds mad, but it's as if the skyline has changed. How can a skyline change?'

I spoke next. 'I'm somewhere completely different from you guys. All I can see is the Middle East and oil.'

That was all, we saw no more and had no idea what any of it meant. At the time we thought we had got our wires crossed; it had just been a bad session. We gave up, deflated, believing we had been unsuccessful.

Since that experience, we have heard of many other people having similar premonitions about 9/11 but we had no idea this was happening – how could we have known? We just thought we had come up with a lot of nonsense which didn't make sense. We still had no answers as to why we had come together. We were lost and I had no idea what our next move should be or which way we should turn. We were expecting some big revelation from our session about our own past lives and thought it had been a waste of time. In hindsight, we now know that we glimpsed one of the biggest and most shocking events the world has known.

Two weeks later I received a call from Dave at my office.

'Have you heard?'

'Heard what?' I replied, confused.

'It's happening, everything we saw in the session is happening. Steve and I are at work transfixed by the television, watching everything we saw happen.'

I logged onto to the web and went to Sky News. My blood ran cold as I saw the very scenes Steve and Dave had described. Suddenly, we understood what the session had been about and why I had seen the Middle East. Our three visions had seemed unconnected but now we knew better: we had jumped forward in time.

The big breakthrough

Without realising it, that group regression had been the first of many Future Life Progression sessions. I knew that this was the beginning of something big but I had no idea what it was or why it was happening to me. I was inspired – it felt like I was on the brink of a great discovery, and I began experimenting with willing clients, myself, my friends and the soldiers. I began by taking individuals forward five and ten years into the future to discover where they were living, who was in their life and how their careers had panned out. Some even saw their own children and grandchildren. But would their futures come about just as they had seen in their future life progressions?

Soon the phone calls and emails came, telling me that my clients had found the house they had seen themselves living in, or that they had just been for an interview at the office they had had a vision of working in. Some people had even met the partner they had seen themselves married to in their session. Other clients and friends saw themselves in the future and over their current problems – and had therefore discovered the solution.

Then it hit me: I realised how powerful this process could be in helping people to map out their futures. Not only could clients see what was happening in, say, six months, or six years, they could see how things *would* turn out if they made a particular choice. For example, people could see the type of life they would have if they married a particular partner, went for that job promotion, bought that run-down house that later turned out to be in a property hot spot. The more I explored Future Life Progression, the more I realised what a wonderful tool it is for people taking control of their destiny and creating the reality they want and deserve. Who hasn't thought, 'What would have happened if I had done so and so...?' Future Life Progression takes away the uncertainty of not knowing the outcome – because you can see what happens and then make your decision accordingly. Throughout this book I will show you how to use the process to have a positive impact on every area of your life.

As well as helping my clients to make the right choices, I noticed that something else was happening to people who had Future Life Progression, something I had no explanation for at the time. My clients seemed different after their FLP session. They were more self-assured, more confident and they had more direction about where they were heading. They even walked out of my office in a more self-assured manner. They walked as if they had a purpose.

I continued working with Dave and Steve the soldiers and they made further predictions about what is to come in the world. So far, many of their premonitions have come true.

I took journeys forward into my own future where I saw myself with a property in a city that didn't exist at the time. I later bought a flat in Palm Island, Dubai, that doubled in value. I have also used FLP to check out the location of a new office in London, to see which would be more popular with clients, and have even used it to check out whom I should work with on projects. The information I glean is never wrong.

Myself, the soldiers, friends and clients have also travelled way into the future, to our future lifetimes and the world in 100 years' time. Time and time again, the participants came up with the same scenarios, but let me tell you this – I have seen the future of our world and the human race, and what I have seen has made me very optimistic. By the time you have read this book not only will you feel the same, but you will also have discovered how to travel forward in time and find out all you need to know about your own future.

Everything you need to know about Future Life Progression

Before you begin your exciting journey through time and space, here are answers to some of the many questions you may have regarding FLP.

Q: How far into the future can I see?
A: It's entirely up to you. In Future Life Progression sessions I usually take my clients five and ten years into their futures and then into their next lifetime. I feel that these time frames provide the best answers. Most things you need to know right now will be answered by looking at five years' time, such as where you are working, who you are with or where you are living.

As you will learn from the many case studies in this book, we all have different needs – some people need to look at their next lifetime, others may simply need to see where they are in two years' time. It is possible to look as far ahead as 1,000

years, if you want to, but most people who come to me for
sessions are concerned with their life now.

Q: What is a future lifetime?

A: Most of you will have heard of past lives, when you have
incarnated before to experience lives as diverse as a peasant
in medieval England to a singer in the 1950s. Future Life
Progression works along the same lines as Past Life
Regression, except that instead of travelling into the past you
travel into the future. In this book you will also come across
the term 'higher self', this is the part of you (the energy)
which knows all and is connected to the universe — sometimes referred to as your 'higher guide.' During Future Life
Progression, your higher self provides the answers to your
questions and links you with your future lifetimes. Think of
your higher self as an experienced pilot ready and waiting to
help you take off into the future.

Q: Why do I need to see the future?

A: A surprising number of people have asked me this question.
By seeing the future you can make better decisions, you can
discover which direction to go in, where to buy property, what
school to send your children to, who will be a negative influence in your life and who a positive one. You can identify which
jobs or businesses will be good moves.

Q: Is the future set?

A: No. We all create our own destiny and that's one of the
big secrets in life. I don't think that you have just one future,
one destiny. I believe that life is like being on a huge
motorway and at each junction are choices. You decide which

Logical thinking

A common reaction to FLP is that the logical side of the brain tries to make sense of what we see during a progression. Somehow our brain tells us this can't be right – we cannot see the future, can we? So the brain tries to find a rational answer to what is happening. This is why clients during an FLP session very often comment, 'I must be imagining this. I must be seeing this because this is what I fear or because this is what I want.' Others will think, 'This must be something I've read in a book or seen in a film.' The key to success with FLP is to just flow and let whatever you see just take shape in your mind without resistance. If you start to analyse it you will break the stream of information.

junction, which decisions to make, and these take you onto different routes. With FLP you will be able to find out what will happen if you take a particular course of action. In short, you will be able to see your different futures and then choose which you feel is best for you.

Q: Is FLP safe?

A: In over 20 years since I've been doing Past Life Regression, conducting hundreds of sessions, no one has had a bad reaction to either PLR or later on, to FLP. It's a very simple process – I put my client into a relaxed state and I put plenty of protection around them by imagining a beautiful white light around them. To do this, I use suggestions such as, 'You will learn what you need to learn from this session. You are safe and protected.' Before each exercise I also suggest that you open up and close down (see page 00 for a full explanation). All experienced psychics, and spiritual workers, follow a practice of opening up to link into the universe and shutting down after completing their work, so they are not open psychically. This is standard practice and one that I strongly advise you get into the habit of doing before any spiritual work. I will give you a gentle reminder to open up and close down after each exercise in this book.

Q: Will I be in a trance?

A: During a session you will be in a comfortably relaxed state similar to when you are engrossed in a good movie or daydreaming.

Q: Will I see anything bad?

A: There is no need to see anything negative unless it is something you can change. With most people, if we look ten years into the future it's possible that an elderly relative would have passed away or someone we know would have suffered a car crash or illness. There would be no point in seeing any of these things unless you could do something about them. You may see yourself in a relationship that is going nowhere or a dead-end job, because this gives you the power to not take that route and to make different choices now to change your destiny. You can even look at alternative futures with FLP to find out which works out the best. But ultimately, you will only see future events that you can influence now, in the present.

Q: Supposing I am no longer alive in ten years' time?

A: In my early days of working with FLP I was concerned that someone would find that they had passed over before the ten-year point. I made a pact with the universe not to bring anyone to me or my therapists who would not survive this time frame. I do not think it serves any purpose for anyone to know they will be passing over soon unless, as I mentioned earlier, they can change things. Also, I've always stayed clear of predicting health problems because there are so many factors involved in creating health issues and if the illness does come to fruition, or not, either way knowing you or a loved one may fall ill can cause unnecessary distress. As I believe in working on a positive energy level, I don't wish to place a piece of worrying information into someone's mind.

Q: Can I do the exercises alone?

A: There are a number of ways of conducting the exercises. You can get a friend to talk you through each one, or you can record the exercises on to a tape or CD. You can also download many of the exercises from my website on to your ipod or MP3. Visit **www.futurelifeprogression.com**

Q: Does everyone see something?

A: We are all different and we all have different experiences. I can never tell anyone what or how they will experience FLP, but the vast majority of people do gain information of their future in some form or other.

Q: What will I see?

A: Most people will see some sort of image. Some people see a mini movie, others see a fleeting still image. The key is to acknowledge whatever comes to you. If you stop and think, 'Oh that wasn't much,' or 'that cannot be right' you stop the flow. I actually see an energy above my clients head, which tells me that the information is arriving. I then see it begin to flow, and as my clients relate what is coming to them the information flows more and more.

However, some individuals are not very visual. Instead, they may have very strong feelings and just 'know' what is happening. They will say things like, 'I don't know why, but I feel I'm living in Spain', or 'I get the feeling I am married to a lovely man but I do not know what he looks like.' Now this doesn't mean you cannot find out what something or someone looks like; you can simply ask yourself, 'What do I feel he is like? Tall or short? Dark or fair?' The answers will flow.

As you go through the exercises in *The Future Is Yours* you will discover which is your dominant sense but, as a guideline, think about your last holiday. Think in detail about what you liked and disliked about your trip. Now think of three words to describe it.

Get a piece of paper and write down the three words *now*.

◆ If you jotted down words such as 'beautiful' or 'great scenery', or find yourself describing images, then you are more visual

◆ If you use words such as 'relaxing', 'warm' or 'peaceful' then you are more feeling

◆ If you find yourself mentioning the sounds of the waves, or the music or any other noises, then you are more auditory. It's not common, but some people do hear their future. They can hear words in their mind, as if someone were communicating with them telepathically, or they may even hear someone whispering in their ear

Q: Are there any other ways in which people relay information in FLP?

A: Some people have a big chunk of information pop into their heads. This is very common in business people. They are fascinating to work with – they sound as if they are reading from a book as they relay a constant flow of facts, figures and future trends in business. FLP is excellent for pinpointing changes in any market place, be it food, fashion or flowers.

Q: What if there is no improvement in my future, or if things have got worse?

A: Then we can look at alternate futures, there are always options. This is the beauty of FLP – you can access your mistakes now before you re-experience them in this life. As touched on earlier, I believe that alternative futures exist and are waiting for us – depending on the choices that we make *right now*. If you were to throw this book out of the window and ignore the advice I'm going to give you in the remaining chapters, your life would take a very different path. Discarding this book is an example of how at each moment, through our actions, we change our future destiny. FLP allows you to see the possibilities of what will happen if you follow a particular path – you tap into, and experience, your future reality.

Our four future lives

From years of experience progressing people into their future lives, I've come to the conclusion that we have four alternative futures, four possible paths to follow. On each path there are turnings set by fate which take us onto another journey. This is how I believe this play we call life works: fate sets up events, chance meetings and experiences depending on how we *choose* to react (which is our free will) and we are then bumped onto another life path. In a way, I think we are constantly shifting between these four lives. Think of the saying, 'I'm back on track' and you will grasp the idea. Our actions determine which path we take and the outcome of our lives. In essence, we have to take responsibility for how our lives turn out and FLP helps you to do this because it gives you the confidence to make the right choices.

Q: What if I do not see any improvement for a very long time?
A: This is a really good question and probably one of the most important. Over the years I have noticed something wonderful happen. FLP speeds up positive energy – it attracts a good vibe, and the good parts of the future happen sooner! There is no way that you won't see an improvement for a very long time. By using Future Life Progression you will be tapping into the universal energy to *create* a better future for yourself. While practising one of the FLP techniques in this book you may glimpse lives that are disastrous as a result of wrong choices, but you will find the right 'ending' or solution to a problem, or the right way on your path at that particular moment. And by

tapping into the positive creative energy of the universe you will speed up events, coincidences or synchronicity, to make this happen.

Case study

One of my friends used the Thinking out of the Box technique, (see page 147) to find out if she would ever fulfil her dream of buying a holiday home by the seaside. She saw herself in a gorgeous flat, just minutes from the sea front. She called me and said, 'Anne, I've no idea how I will make it happen as I hardly have time to eat, let alone find the right property two hours from where I live.' I told her to put it into the hands of the universe. Two weeks later, the woman went to stay at a small seaside town on business. She discovered that the owner of the guest house she had chosen to stay at was married to a mortgage broker. 'I couldn't believe it when he told me he could sort out my second mortgage for no fee, register me with all the local estate agents and recommend a list of tradespeople for any renovation work,' my friend confided. The cynics among you might think that this was all too easy, and she was going to be ripped off – but she wasn't. She went with her gut instinct and the broker turned out to be helpful and honest. He now acts as an agent for the property which is a holiday let – he advised her to rent out the flat for part of the year, which means this way her holiday home pays for itself! This story is a good example of how after a session positive events can unfold very quickly. This will happen to you, too; your FLP vision will soon become reality.

Q: How will I feel after my FLP experience?

A: I have come across people who have mentioned feeling light-headed when they have taken part in guided imagery or visualization. By learning to open up and close down properly before and after the exercises (see pages 42 and 44) you will avoid light-headedness; you will also feel fresh and alert, and able to gain the right information during the exercises.

Case study

Celia married young and had two children before she was 20. When her marriage broke up she was the sole breadwinner and worked tirelessly to keep the home together. Now she was stuck in a dead-end job and could see no way out. She needed the money to keep the home going and had no time to study. She told me, 'By the time the children are off my hands it will be a bit late to start a new career.'

I took Celia forward five years and little had changed – only now, the children were bigger and more expensive. Her earnings had not risen in line with her expenses. If anything, life was even harder. Celia gave a sigh as I took her forward ten years from the present time. 'Why bother?" she protested, 'My life will be even more of a drag by then.'

Yet as she arrived at her ten-year future, a lovely warm glow came over her. She said, 'Wow, I am certainly not in the dreary office now. I am in some sort of a shop. No, wait, it is a salon. I am massaging a lady's hands. I look very smart.'

'How long have you been working there?' I asked.

'Two years.'

'And how did you manage to make the transition from the office to this new job?'

'I saved £5 a week and did little courses on waxing and facials. Then I continued to save cash and took some bigger courses. A lot were at night school, one evening a week. My dad watched the boys for me and because I was on a low income, the courses cost next to nothing, so even on my rubbish salary I could still afford them.'

'Could you start on these courses sooner?'

'Well yes, I could,' Celia replied. 'It never occurred to me. I have been feeling so stuck that I couldn't see a way out, but now I can see that this would work. I will have to have a little chat to my dad and check out the night schools.'

Celia called me a few months later. She sounded so much happier as she enthused, 'I have just finished my first course and I want to thank you by offering you a complementary nail treatment. I'm so glad I didn't have to wait so long for my life to change. FLP showed me what to do.'

Since working with FLP I have heard many similar stories. My clients travel forward to discover how they have overcome problems, or to find out what they will finally be doing. They find the answers to see if relationships have worked out, and if not why not, and who they are with if it's someone else. They have even gone forward and downloaded the information they need such as the theme to a book or play, a successful song and many other skills relating to work and pleasure.

In two places at once

There is a misconception that when we go into an altered state, such as meditation or hypnosis, our conscious mind shuts down or goes somewhere else. In actual fact it's a little bit like driving – you're concentrating on the road and you're aware of what is happening but at the same time you can be deep in thought. You have probably experienced driving a distance and not remembering how you arrived at your destination because you were miles away, yet you didn't drive through a red light or run anyone over. The conscious mind has taken a bit of a back seat but is ready to jump into action at any moment. While you're experiencing FLP your subconscious mind is accessing the future but your conscious mind is still present. This conscious mind is the chattering part of your brain, and whilst you are experiencing your future with FLP, and what I call the Process, your conscious will be trying to make sense of it.

How to use this book

In the coming chapters you will discover all you need to know about FLP.

In Chapter 2, Do You Have the Time? – read about how scientists have proven that time doesn't work the way we think it does, and how you can play with time, even speeding it up or slowing it down at will.

In Chapter 3, Love is in the Air! You will learn how to see who is in your life or even if they are still around you in your next lifetime. You will discover, using FLP, how to make the best love choices for a happy union which benefits both you and your partner. You will also see case studies of people who have found love and seen their future partners during a session – and then met them.

Chapters 4 and 5 relate case studies of people who have used FLP to find which business ventures will work and which are dead ducks. You will even discover how some clients have received warnings which have saved them from financial disaster, along with how to use FLP to make wise choices regarding investments.

How do you understand your own patterns and life path? Chapters 6, 7 and 8 relate to you and your life path, and show you how to look at alternative futures and decide which is best for you. You will be able to move forward in time and find out how you resolved a current problem. You will see who and where you are in your future lifetime, discovering who you have evolved into, and how the life you are living now will shape the future you. You will tap into the wisdom of the future you, accessing your own highly evolved energy.

Later, in Chapter 9, I look at the world and how it is in 100 years' time through my own study into the future. This research has been carried out in groups: I held workshops and guided visualizations with people at my offices, and also used a guided session on CD. The session has been sent out all over the globe – and the major response is that the world is a better place.

The study reveals which countries have prospered and which are struggling. You will find out how you will travel in the future, what you will wear, what you will eat and how you will power your home and vehicles. You will also be able to take part in future studies.

Keeping a Journal

The exercises included throughout the book are designed to access different information about your future. As you progress through each exercise, you will find that some are easier than others, so don't worry if you do not connect with all of them. You may find that some suit you more at different times in your life depending on what you need to know right then and there. Most people find they get better and clearer information from the techniques with practise.

As you work through this book, keep a journal so you can record your FLP sessions. This will give you confidence in the technique because you will have written proof when your FLP sessions later become a reality, and in this way your journal will also act as a progress record.

You notes should include:

◆ What you saw

◆ Feelings

◆ Key words, numbers and dates that you can recall from the session

You may find that your questions change over time but by keeping a note of your answers you will gain greater insight and awareness of your needs.

You have not discovered this book by chance. Simply possessing it is a sign that you are ready to step forward into your own future, to grow and evolve and to make the world a better place.

So come with me on an amazing journey in the future – your future.

CHAPTER 2
Do You Have the Time?

Having practised as a tarot consultant for around 30 years, I have predicted the future on a daily basis. Yet when I discovered Future Life Progression my mind was filled with questions about how this process could be possible. As a result, I began a quest and my own FLPs led me to investigate if anyone else had undergone similar experiences. I was curious to see what, if anything, other people had seen of their future incarnations.

I discovered that the concept of Future Life Progression is not as new as many people think. Psychic Edgar Cayce, who died in 1945, claimed to have dreamt about his next incarnation in Nebraska in the year 2100 AD, when the sea covered all of the Western part of America. Cayce predicted that in this next lifetime he would remember his previous incarnation as Edgar Cayce who had lived 200 years before. In his future vision he saw a group of scientists visiting his previous homes with him after travelling there in a long, cigar-shaped metal flying ship that moved at high speed.

Time travellers: Wambach and Snow

The first scientist to study Future Life Progression was psychologist Dr Helen Wambach who in the mid-1960s began regressing people into their past lives – her aim was to disprove regression. Over a ten-year period of past-life recalls, using hypnosis with 1,088 people, she amassed a huge amount of data and asked participants key questions about their lives, even down to details such as what they ate, wore and their role in their community. She concluded that, with the exception of 11 participants, their descriptions of clothing, footwear utensils, money and housing, for example, were consistent with historical records.

Later, Wambach began progressing her subjects into their next lifetimes, after she found that people spontaneously jumped forward in time just as I had discovered. Her new techniques were so successful that she began progressing huge groups throughout America and France. She discovered that nine out of ten people gave the same details about who was in government, wars and other key information when she took them to the same point in the future.

Wambach suffered poor health and before her work was concluded she passed away on 18 August 1985, her 60th birthday. A student of hers, Dr. Chet Snow, took up where she left off. Snow had initially visited Wambach because he was writing a book about foretelling the future. He could find no reason for his bouts of writer's block, and had heard that Wambach had helped many people clear problems through Past Life Regression. Snow turned out to be a good subject, and so Wambach asked him to be a subject for FLP.

We have four different futures

Through his own research, Snow discovered that people are able to see four different futures – which I agree with too, after working with many clients – and from this he came to the conclusion that the future is not fixed. His theory puts forward the concept that we can change events and that instead of focussing on the negative aspects, such as war and tidal waves, we should focus on building a better world – on the positive. His studies were published four years after Wambach's death in his book *Mass Dreams of the Future*.

Since 1977, Dr Bruce Goldberg, author of *Past Lives, Future Lives*, who holds degrees in biology, chemistry and dentistry, has worked extensively in this field as a hypnotherapist with more than 35,000 people.

As I studied the works of these eminent people and brilliant thinkers, I realised that it was obvious that if we have had lives before then surely we will have lives in the future beyond the life we are in right now.

Running parallel to my quest to find out if anyone else had experienced FLP was a thirst to find out how time worked. Again, I kept on coming back to the question: how can you really accurately see things which haven't yet occurred? With so many ideas floating around in my mind, I set out to find some more answers. I read books, went to lectures and surfed the internet. But despite having proof that people had experienced FLP, I was still struggling to understand the basics of time. However, I discovered that the vast majority of people, including the experts, also struggled with the concepts surrounding time. In fact, many quantum physicists have gone grey trying to understand time, the universe and how it all works. American physicist and Nobel prize winner Richard

Feynman admitted in *A Life in Science*, 'It is safe to say that nobody understands quantum mechanics.'

All the eminent experts can be sure of is that time doesn't work the way we think it does, which is why when people first hear about FLP they look confused. Their first thoughts are, 'This can't possibly work, how can we see something that hasn't happened yet?' The concept seems to raise more questions such as:

◆ If we can see the future then can we change it?

◆ How does time work and indeed what is time?

◆ If time doesn't run in a straight line then what does it do?

After working with my clients, and taking my own trips, I am convinced we can jump time and see into the future. However, if I simply claim that time doesn't run in a straight line, and you can jump in and out of the past and future, that probably wouldn't be enough for you. This is why I'm going to explain the various theories of time and how it works in the coming pages. By grasping how time works you will start to feel more comfortable with FLP and see that it really is a reality – if you can free your mind.

Creating a Belief System

The first step on our journey is finding out where our beliefs come from – how do we create them? Imagine if you were alive centuries ago when people believed the earth was flat, and then someone came along and told you the earth was round and you could sail right around it. Would you have ridiculed them?

We like to believe that we think for ourselves but in actual fact most of our beliefs have been given to us. Few people do not share the same religious and political views as their parents, and many take on board the beliefs held by their family and peers without questioning these ideas.

One thing I've noticed after years of attending lectures and workshops is that people become very upset when their beliefs are challenged, a point made in Michael Talbot's *The Holographic Universe* where it says that people 'behave like addicts' if you question their beliefs. Few people will stop and say, 'Actually you may have a point there.' Instead, they become irrationally angry. Karl Marx was aware of this when he commented, 'Religion is the opium of the masses.'

Throughout civilisation people have had all sorts of beliefs, many of which we would laugh at today. It is easy to mock, yet many individuals don't question where their beliefs originate or why they continue to cling to them – including how they view time.

A friend of mine, Bridget, told me about growing up in Ireland. One day she put her hat on the table and her dad shouted at her, 'Get that hat off the table, it is unlucky.' She told me, 'In my childish innocence I asked him how it could possible be unlucky. A look of realisation came across his face. He had never thought about it before.' He told her that his dad had always shouted if anyone had put a hat on the table. So the next time she saw her granddad she asked him why he had this reaction. He replied, 'Well, as kids we often had fleas so we weren't allowed to put our hats on the table.' This story is a good example of how beliefs become patterns which can then be unconsciously handed down through generations.

In his book *Entangled Minds,* scientist Dean Radin poses the question 'Can beliefs distort common sense?' He cites the case of British physician William Harvey who in 1628 looked at a heart and saw something that others had missed. Until that time it was thought that everything that was to be known on the subject of medicine had been written by Greek anatomist Claudius Galen. Galen had written that the human heart was a heater and the brain a cooler. But William Harvey had noticed that the heart looked rather like a pump attached to a circulatory system. Now this all seems obvious to you and I, but we have been brought up to understand that the heart pumps blood around the body. When Harvey proposed his ideas to colleagues they thought the theory ridiculous. Harvey claimed he could hear the heart beating, but they simply couldn't hear it. A leading medical doctor of the time, Emilio Parisano of Venice, said, 'He claims that this movement (of blood round arteries) produces a pulse, and, moreover, a sound. That sound, however, we deaf people cannot hear, and there is no one in Venice who can.' It's easy to see why no other doctors in Venice could grasp the concept being posed by Harvey. As Radin says in his book, 'Beliefs can easily cause us to become blind to the obvious.' I'm asking now that you suspend everything you have thought about how time works and read on with an open mind.

The Beliefs Surrounding Time

We construct our reality on various factors including what we experience with our senses (see, hear, taste, smell and feel) and our perception of the passage of time. Yet no one seems to truly know how time works. All we have is a collection of theories that no one, ie lay people and the experts (physicists), can agree on – except one thing. Everyone agrees that time is not linear, in other words the past is not behind us and the future is not in front of us.

In a letter to the family of his lifelong friend Besso, who had just died, Albert Einstein once commented, 'For us believing physicists, the distinction between past, present and future is only an illusion, even if a stubborn one.' When you first hear this concept that time does not run in a straight line, your mind will be thrown into a spin! You may have been brought up to believe that time is linear; this is a hard fact as sure as the sun rises every morning and sets every evening. It was some time before I could get my head around this fact too but once I did my next question was the same as everyone else's. If time isn't running in a straight line, how does it work? If yesterday wasn't yesterday or somewhere behind us, then where is it?

Hold on tight, because whatever you believe about time is about to be smashed into pieces, thrown up in the air and vanish in a cloud of smoke.

How Scientists Measure Time

We live with the illusion that time is somehow moving in a straight line from past to present to future. The majority of people think that they began this life at birth then move forward through childhood, then teens, adulthood, middle years, old age, then finally death. They watch the ever-ticking clock that tells them it is time to get up or go to work, eat lunch or go to bed.

They think that time can be measured. But if time can be

measured then it must always be the same length, surely? Yet this is not true at all. Time speeds up and it slows down.

Einstein believed that time was relative – that it actually flowed faster and slower according to your circumstances. He argued that if you were enjoying yourself time would move faster. The genius himself joked, 'When you sit with a nice girl for two hours, it seems like two minutes. When you sit on a hot stove for two minutes, it seems like two hours – that's relativity.' The physicist also proved that when a moving object's speed nears the speed of light, time would run slower relative to a stationary object. He used an example of two clocks, one moving and one still. He stated that the moving clock, travelling at an enormous speed would tick more slowly than the clock that remained still.

But there is more. Not only does time run at different speeds for moving or stationary objects, it also runs at different speeds in different places. It is hard to believe, but scientists have proven this beyond doubt. It has also been proved that gravity can stretch or slow down time; the stronger the gravitational field the more time is slowed down, relative to an observer further away from the source of gravity (like our own planet). Time has also been measured to run at minutely different speeds, in an experiment by Robert Pound and Glen Rebka at Harvard University in 1959. Their results proved that our intuitive view of time is not the same as how it really works. Time is elastic.

Speeding Up and Slowing Down Time

We have all experienced time running at different speeds. The day of my daughter's wedding last year flashed by in the blink of an eye. I still puzzle how so much could happen and yet the entire day seemed to last an hour. From getting up to getting ready, picking up guests, travelling to the church, the entire service, travelling to the reception, speeches, food, drinks, chatting to dozens of people until the early hours of the following morning. Yet I could swear all these events took less than a couple of hours.

A few days later, I had a meeting with my bank manger who kept me waiting and waiting. I was painfully bored. I looked through my dairy to check my appointments, sent a few text messages, wrote some notes and still I sat there waiting. I huffed and puffed and glared at the girl on the counter. Then flicked through a magazine, sent another text and eventually he appeared. When I looked at my watch he was just seven minutes late. To me it was an eternity.

We have all experienced time being elastic – depending on our emotions and perception. Another good example is that if we have no time limit something simple, like cleaning out the cupboard under the stairs, can be stretched out to fill an entire day. Yet when the pressure is on we can achieve ten times the work that we normally do to meet a tight deadline.

Years ago a neighbour of mine, let's call her Sally, demonstrated this perfectly. She had a happy-go-lucky personality and her home reflected her character. It was always nice to pop in and see her and everyone who did relaxed immediately, even though they would have to remove an apple core and an old newspaper before sitting down.

One day the neighbour had a phone call from her mother-in-law to say she was on her way to visit – unexpectedly. We looked around at the pile of ironing, discarded coffee cups, magazines, ashtrays and biscuits trodden into the carpet. For one second we glanced at the chaos, then without a word we both leapt into action.

Twenty minutes later her mother-in-law walked into the house and there we were, coffee in hand, sitting in an immaculate living room discussing the news of the day. We had tidied, vacuumed, polished and cleared away what would normally have taken both of us a day to sort out.

Admittedly if the visitor had peeped behind the sofa she would have found a pile of assorted items that had been hidden there – and the last two days' washing up was hidden in the oven. But this incident taught me two things: firstly, never let your mother-in-law visit without proper notice and, secondly, amazing things can happen in a short space of time when you want them to, and you are open to the idea.

In the next exercise you will practise how to speed up and slow down time yourself.

Fast and Slow Time

◆ Stop and think of when time has passed very slowly or even seemed to stand still. Maybe waiting in the dentist or for a train? Perhaps being somewhere excruciatingly boring? Remember what it felt like. Really be aware of time moving slowly.

◆ Now think back to when time flashed past. You were probably having lots of fun and with people you really liked. Notice how you felt. Notice how much happened in that space of time.

◆ Contrast how the two felt. Notice how when time moved

slowly it seemed to almost stand still, and when it moved quickly it seemed to flash past.

◆ Now when you need the minutes to pass slowly, such as when you need more time to get something finished, remind yourself of the slow time feeling. Really bring the feeling inside of you by tapping into the emotion you recalled earlier. Slow down your breathing, and actually slow down your thinking and talking, even your internal dialogue. You will find that somehow time has stretched.

◆ Using the same idea in reverse, the next time you need time to go quickly, bring up the fast time feeling that you tapped into earlier in this exercise. Bring the feeling to the surface and at the same time allow your thinking to become faster. Do the same with your speech, including your internal dialogue – focus on times when thing have moved quickly and suddenly you will find time passing by in an instant.

If you have ever been in a car crash, or another kind of serious accident, you may have experienced the whole incident either passing in a flash or in slow motion.

One of my clients once witnessed a robbery in shop. To her everything happened in slow motion to the extent that every single word that was spoken sounded like a CD on slow speed. The robbers broke a window and even the glass appeared to fly through the air almost like a series of separate pictures slowly flowing one after the other. She was amazed by the experience, and this is yet another example of how time can be speeded up or slowed down according to your 'time frame.' The more you learn about time, the more surprises you will find. Many people who accept that we can see the future are surprised when they discover they can change the speed of time as you have just done in the above exercise. Even fewer people would believe that we can actually change the past.

'What we call the past is information and what we call the future is formed by the laws of probability, intent consciousness and present activities. In short, the past, present and future appear to exist at the same time in a multidimensional reality.'

F.Holmes 'Skip' Atwater

The next exercise on page 43, Back to the Future, will get you into the habit of moving around in time. By going back to your past self, you will see just how much you would have benefited from a visited of the current you. Ten years ago you had needs, you had questions, you had dilemmas and problems. Know how much wiser you are now and how much you can help your past self.

Once you have completed this exercise you will realise just how much you will benefit when you meet the future you, your future self, who will in turn help and advise you.

But before you try this exercise I would like you to do the opening up technique and after the exercise, you need to carry out the closing down technique (see pages 42,44). Opening up and closing down will protect and ground you and help you to gain the most for your experiences of travelling into the future.

....

Opening Up

The opening up technique is the perfect preparation for each exercise. It will relax you in mind and body, protect you and connect you to your higher self. It needs to be done before you do any of the exercises in each chapter, it will take you just a few moments.

◆ Find yourself a comfy place to settle. Really sink into the bed or chair or wherever you find yourself. Now take a few long deep breaths and each time you breath in think the word love and with each breath out think the word release.

◆ As you breathe in and out know that you are releasing any negative thoughts, feelings and emotions allowing you to gain knowledge that you need to know for your own benefit. As you breath in you will be breathing in a loving positive energy.

◆ Now imagine a white light shining down on you protecting you and surrounding you with love. The white light will stay with you throughout your exercise.

◆ Know that the white light is connected to the universal energy that knows all. Every single piece of information is stored here and you will now have access to that information. Allow it to flow to you and bring you what you need to know.

....

....

Back to the Future

Imagine if you could go back ten years and have a word with yourself. Think back to what you were doing ten years ago. What was happening in your life? What were you struggling with? What did you need to know? You now have the benefit of hindsight. Take time over this exercise.

♦ Think carefully: what advice would you give yourself? What changes would you make and how would they affect you now?

♦ Now think about how far you have come in that time. How you have grown. What have you learnt? What was hard for you then that is easy for you now?

♦ Now imagine you have actually travelled back ten years in time. The you of ten years past is now standing in front of you. What would you advise yourself to do? What moves would you suggest making? What would you say is a waste of time and what is worth going for immediately?

♦ Are there any people you would tell yourself to avoid, or to connect with?

♦ What skills have you developed since? What have you improved at? What areas of your life are you more confident in?

♦ What do you know now that you wished you had known them? What situations were a problem then but are not a problem now?

Very soon as you progress onto the next chapters you will be going forward ten years – only this time the future you, in the form of your higher self, will be giving you advice. Now you can have the benefit of hindsight, up front.

Closing Down

Closing down after each exercise will ground you and bring you back down to earth. You will be able to process the information that you have just gained whilst feeling strong and focussed and ready to carry on your day.

◆ After each exercise allow your breathing to become regular and feel the white light slowly drawing back towards the universe. It has done its job – it has looked after you.

◆ Notice that a little of the white light still remains around you shimmering. It will protect you and keep you safe and if at any time you need more universal love and protection it will draw more to you but for now this is all you need. A slight shimmer of light.

◆ Finally, imagine yourself reconnecting with your everyday life feeling your feet on the ground and your body strong. Now feel ready to move forward with confidence with your new knowledge and energy to guide you.

Please remember to open up and close down after every exercise which now follows in this book.

Believing in yourself

The following case study illustrates how Future Life Progression can give you belief in your talents and dreams. Many people don't reach their full potential because they let go of their aspirations as a result of being afraid of failure. FLP will show you how you can reach your goal.

Many of the Future Life Progression methods you will learn are similar – they all use some trigger that takes you into the future. However, the techniques all have a different twist to them that is relevant to the particular area I'm discussing – for example, love, work or investments. In Philip's case I used the method that I call The Gallery (see page 52) as this is the first technique I teach my students because it's easy to use and quick to learn. Hopefully by reading Philip's story you will begin to grasp FLP's power as a tool for transforming your own life.

Case study

Philip had always wanted to be an actor. As a child he would make up his own plays and even managed to get a lead part in the school play. He dreamed of life in films and on stage, but his family persuaded him to get a 'real' career first as a safety net.

Philip told me, 'I don't need a safety net. I know I can act and I know I can make it but I suppose my dad has a point. Supposing it takes me years to make it or supposing I do well then fizzle out? Around 70 per cent of actors are out of work as my dad is forever telling me. I need to know when I will make it so that I know how much I need to be prepared. If it isn't going to happen for ten years or more, then I had better do as my dad says.'

I explained to Philip that if success as an actor was in his future he wouldn't need to wait for the full length of time. Once he had seen his future he could bring it to himself sooner. Philip shrugged and I could see he had no idea what I was talking about. This didn't matter because I knew he would understand once he had experienced FLP – as you will too.

So, I took Philip forward five years using The Gallery and he said, 'I'm looking at the pictures on the gallery wall and it's like watching a film of myself. I can see that I am working in my father's business. He is thrilled but I am bored out of my mind. I'm doing the accounts. This is not what I wanted to see at all.'

'Is anything happening to do with acting?' I asked.

'I don't get a lot of time but I have just got myself an agent. He is a kindly old chap who is telling me he can get me plenty of work. I just wish I wasn't so bogged down. It seems to have taken me a long time to get just this far.'

It was time to look a bit further into the future. I took Philip forward another five years as I wanted to see where he was ten years from his current time.

He beamed, 'I am on stage. I have a lead role. This is fantastic.'

'Are you still working for your dad?'

'No. I stopped that years ago.'

I then prompted Philip to ask his future self for any advice on how he could achieve his dream. The reply came back, 'Philip, if you know you are that good why are you listening to your father?'

Philip gave a wry smile. His self in the future, his future self, had hit the nail on the head. I then asked, 'And are you still with the same agent, the kindly elderly man?'

His successful future self, Philip in ten years time, replied, 'No not at all, he was a lot of hot air. Now I am with a young agency in London, they're really backing me and using their contacts to get me work.'

After the session Philip looked as if a weight had been lifted off him. 'I think I will pass on the safety net. I'm not going to need it after all,' he said, adding, 'and I will be getting myself a new agent, too.'

The last I heard from Philip he had landed a small role in a television series. He was on his way to stardom. I told him, 'I want a front row seat at your first stage production.'

'You got it,' he replied.

Philip's story is an excellent way of illustrating how you can bring your good future towards you. In his progression, he discovered that he eventually 'made it' around the ten-year mark after leaving his father's firm and changing his agent. For him, these two factors were the crucial actions he needed to move his life forward. Once he had this information, what he had to do to succeed, he decided to act sooner. In short, he brought success to himself more quickly as a result of his taking action. In spiritual terms, Philip speeded up his own destiny –

it was going to happen anyway, but by giving the universe a hand and taking a proactive approach the pieces of the jigsaw came together sooner for him.

Don't wait - bring the future forward

By looking into a future using this safe, and tried and tested process you will be better informed and in a position to make better life choices. You can stop wasting time and bring things forward to you, you will learn how to do this later in the book, so you don't to wait years for what you want in order to have a fulfilling life and achieve your spiritual growth. You will be given the tools to discover which people will be reliable and who will let you down.

Personally, I use Future Life Progression constantly to find out what areas I need to concentrate on with my work and what areas to put to one side. Over the years I have been offered numerous regular radio spots and because of FLP I've known which ones were a waste of time and which have turned out to be beneficial. I have used FLP to discover the right place to have my office. I need to be in a peaceful and positive environment. When my last office building needed to be demolished I used FLP to discover the perfect venue for my work. I am now based in a haven by the River Thames. Occasionally I work in other areas and I tap into how the venue will be in the future and find out if it is suitable.

Next, I'm going to show you how to use the process to find clarity in probably the most important area of you life – love.

CHAPTER 3
Love is in the Air

At one of my recent workshops I asked the participants, 'If I could wave a magic wand and answer any question for you about love, what would you want to know? The answers came back thick and fast:

◆ Will I meet 'the one'?

◆ Will I be with my current partner in the future?

◆ Can I move on from this break-up?

◆ How do I choose between two lovers?

◆ Am I with a commitment phobic?

◆ Can I change this dead-end relationship?

◆ Will my partner ever settle down?

◆ Can I overcome my grief?

This list covers the main questions that clients and participants of my workshops ask me repeatedly. One of the most frequent questions posed in my office from young and old is, 'When will I meet the one?' My clients often apologise for asking, or seem slightly embarrassed, yet who wouldn't want to know something this important? We all want to love and be loved and I don't believe people who say, 'I prefer to be single.' We all want to find out who will be our long-term partner, or, if we are already in a relationship if it will last. If the relationship is difficult, you will also want to know if things will improve.

In fact, who hasn't at some time needed to know where they stand regarding love? If you have managed to get this far in life and not suffered feelings of rejection, hurt, anguish or grief then you are lucky – or have been living like a monk! If your romantic dealings so far have all been plain sailing then believe me, you are an exception.

Whatever it is that you need to know, from seeing if your relationship will last to finding out if your future partner will be good to you – or turn out to be a nightmare – Future Life Progression can answer your questions about love.

My father used to say, 'The best thing in the world is a good marriage, and the worse thing in the world is a bad marriage.' I think he is right. After reading this book, and practising the techniques, you will be able to use FLP to discover whatever it is you need to know about love and romance.

Making a Love List

The first step in learning how to use FLP to overcome your love problems is to identify the problems by making a list. It might seem obvious, but this will help you to focus your mind.

◆ Write a list of questions regarding your love life. These can relate to worries, concerns, problems – any area of your romantic life. You will no doubt find your own issue in the list on the first page of this chapter. I want you to write the issues down, rather than just thinking about them, because by putting pen to paper you are firstly acknowledging them, and secondly sending out a request for help to the universe and to your future self. You are going to learn how to contact your future self, your higher guide, later in this chapter.

◆ Spend some time thinking about your questions.

Now you can move on to The Gallery exercise, which shows you how to find answers to the love questions you most need to know about now.

How The Gallery Works

The Gallery exercise uses the basic techniques of Future Life Progression by allowing you to experience your future – but in a way that doesn't draw you into the emotions. Often people are nervous to look ahead at their love life, you may have this worry too, you may be scared that you won't be with the person that you have feelings for at that moment in time or worry that you will be alone. Don't panic – you will be able to view the picture in The Gallery from a comfortable perspective. While it can be used for any area of your life, I find it particularly useful concerning issues about love because it's so visual. Love is an emotive subject, and The Gallery can help you to make the right choices and find true happiness.

....

The Gallery

Now that you've noted your various love problems, it's time to use FLP to gain instant insight into the issues on your list. The Gallery will help you to access your future, which you will see as a painting. Some people will be able to see photographs if they have a particularly good sense of visualisation.

As you do this exercise, keep your questions at the forefront of your mind. Notice any details that appear because they will be important clues guiding you to make the right decisions.

♦ Begin by using the opening up technique (see page 42).

♦ Find yourself a comfy place to relax, turn off the phone then sink into the chair or bed. Feel your whole body relax and let go as your breathing deepens and you allow time for yourself to answer questions and discover what you need to know.

♦ Allow your breathing to deepen further. As you take each breath in, feel your body being filled with a light and peaceful energy flowing all the way down through your body into your legs and right to the tips of your toes. Then with the next breath feel the peaceful energy flow up to the top of your head, then down the back of your head and spine, as you feel yourself relaxing. Feel any tension floating away with each breath, and with each breath feel your body and mind relax more and more.

♦ Now imagine you are walking along a long tunnel. Feel yourself moving along the tunnel almost floating along, gently gliding. The tunnel is quite dark and is lit by silvery lights either side. As you float along, you notice how the tunnel is quite cool and peaceful. In fact, it's so peaceful you can hear your own breathing, soft and steady and with a slight echo. And as you glide long the tunnel you become more relaxed the further you go, gliding along until you notice up ahead a curtain stretched across the end of the tunnel: a gentle blue velvet cloth. As you float up to the curtain you reach out and pull it to one side.

◆ Behind the soft velvet curtain is a door – a large red shiny door. Notice the shiny red paint. As you run your hand along the smooth surface you see the word 'Gallery.' How big are the letters on the door? Notice how they are made of glistening brass. Trace your fingers around the letters.

◆ Now notice the sturdy brass handle. Reach out, turn the handle, push the door open – and look inside a huge dimly lit room. It is lit by just a few candles and, as your eyes adjust, you notice a candelabra on a solid wooden table. Walk over to the candelabra and light the candles. Now pick up the candelabra and look around the room.

◆ As you look around, you see that the walls are covered in huge paintings. Some are old oil paintings, some are large modern prints and others are faded. Each picture has its own ornate wooden frame. Look around the room and soak in the wondrous atmosphere. Suddenly you are drawn to one particular picture and, as you walk towards it, you realise it is a picture of you with the outcome to the dilemma or question you need to know about.

The answer to whatever you need to know will be here. If you want to know if you will have a child, there will be a picture of you holding your baby. If you want to know if you will get along with your future in-laws, the picture will show you and them. Notice how you all look; are they looking at you and smiling? Do you look happy? Perhaps they are grouped tightly away from you, showing that in the future they will be aloof, or maybe one of them has their back towards you. Notice any expressions on their faces. Most of all, notice your response to them and see if you look happy with the situation.

◆ Maybe you want to know how things will be if you were to marry a particular person. Walk towards the picture and keep your question firmly in your mind. As you arrive at the picture, are they with you or do they not feature in the picture? This tells you that you will not be with this person. Perhaps there is an image of the two of you arm in arm looking very happy or maybe one of you is looking away from the other, showing that you have lost interest.

◆ If you want to know who you will be with in years to come, you will see a picture of yourself in the future. Take time to hook into the image – notice colours, details, shapes. Where are you? Who is around you? How do you feel looking at the picture?

◆ Now step into the picture representing the question you most need to know about. The image is a doorway that holds the key to the future. Focus on the picture, clear your mind of everything else and now step into the picture. Actually feel yourself step inside and take your first impression. How do you feel? What is happening? Do you feel you have made the right moves? Is there any other way you could have handled things? Do you have the best outcome possible for you?

Stay as long as you wish to gain all the information you need. Find out all you need to know. Take your time – there is no rush. Then step out of the picture.

◆ Hold your candelabra high in the air and look at the other pictures. Decide if you want to step inside any of the others. Remember, you can always come back another time by repeating the exercise.

◆ When you are ready put down the candelabra, take one last glance around the room, then walk back through the door and close it behind you. Holding the curtain aside, step into the tunnel. This time as you glide along the corridor, feel at peace – you have the information you need to make the right decisions.

◆ Now find yourself back in your chair or bed refreshed and ready to move forward, making confident moves and knowing exactly what you need to know.

◆ Carry out the closing down technique (see page 44).

You can come back to The Gallery at any time; it is your special place. Don't forget, as your life changes so too will your questions, but The Gallery will still be waiting with answers.

Top tips for using The Gallery

◆ The first time you use The Gallery (page 52) you will automatically travel to the time that will answer your questions. However, you can use The Gallery to go to any point in time, be it six months or six years into the future. Just imagine the period of time you wish to travel to as you begin the visualisation. For example, 'I wish to go six years into the future'.

◆ The Gallery is the perfect exercise for focussing on one specific issue such as, 'Will I get along with my in-laws?' or 'Will my relationship hit a difficult patch?' Or perhaps it will clarify something particular, such as whether you will want children or if you will be happy in another home.

◆ Sometimes there has already been a hint of a problem in a relationship and you may want to go forward and see if it will be an issue in the future, such as a partner drinking too much or being lazy. In such a case, The Gallery will show you the worse you may have to face so that you can either deal with the problem beforehand and change the future, or make the decision as to whether this is something you can live with or not.

Using FLP to Discover 'the One'

As I mentioned at the beginning of this chapter, one of the big issues for clients who are concerned about their love life is wanting to know 'Will I ever meet the one?' FLP is the perfect process to answer this question because it can give you the insight you need and take all the worries and angst out of romance. For someone who has had a bad run of luck in love, finding out that you will meet Mr or Miss Right can bring such happiness. I've helped many people deal with this dilemma and I want to share with you one of my biggest success stories, with one of my clients named Mandy.

Case study

Mandy found her soul mate thanks to a call I received from a journalist who was working for one of the top magazines for women in the UK. The reporter asked me to find a test case so that she could write a feature on my work with FLP. I've a healthy mailing list so I sent out a message asking if anyone would like to take part and the emails came flooding back. However, as soon as I had pressed the send button one of my clients, Mandy, popped into my mind. Over the years I've learnt to listen to my intuition, my psychic nudges, so I sent her a text seeing if she was willing to be an FLP guinea pig.

I have known Mandy since she was a child, watching her grow up through life's trials and tribulations – although she has had more than her fair share. Mandy was beginning to feel that love would pass her by and she was worried. Stunningly good-looking, smart and in a well-paid job she is quite a catch, yet the right man just didn't seem to have crossed her path. She had experienced one serious relation-ship and he had cheated on her with one of her friends. By the time she had finished her education and helped her family through a series of crises, several years had passed and somehow Mandy felt she had missed out on love.

Mandy quickly returned my message and, despite at that point being unclear about how FLP worked, she trusted me and my instincts enough to want to give it a go. The session went very well. Mandy was a great subject, and she soon began describing herself in her kitchen cradling a baby – she realised it was hers. I asked her if she had a husband and she glowed and said, 'He is tall, dark and handsome, just like George Clooney. He is smartly dressed in a blue jumper and grey trousers and he's leaning on the kitchen work top chatting about his day at work.' Mandy went on to tell me that he was a high-powered consultant.

After the session, the reporter interviewed first Mandy, and then me. Three weeks after the session, and before the magazine came out, Mandy went to a wedding, and in walked the very man she had seen in her progression. Excitedly she sent me a text and asked what she should do. I told her, 'Do nothing; just let things take their course.' But by that time the man, named Sat, had spotted her and made a beeline. They talked endlessly and swapped phone numbers and email addresses, within three weeks they had met each others' families and were talking about their future together. Then the magazine was published.

Mandy emailed Sat at work and told him, 'Go and buy *Woman's Own*. She gave no explanation.' One hour after his lunch break he called her up and said, 'I knew the second I saw you that I would marry you. The odd thing is I am wearing the very clothes you described now in your FLP session, a smart blue top and grey trousers.'

Attending their wedding was very special for me, I had seen Mandy find the man of her dreams but I also had concrete proof that FLP worked and gives great benefits to people. The magazine feature brought a flood of people wanting to try their luck and see if they could see how their love life would pan out in the future. Many wanted to know if, like Mandy, they would ever meet Mr or Miss Right, whilst others were keen to discover if the relationships they were in would last.

The Love Boat

This exercise doesn't give you a time frame for when you will meet 'the one'. Its aim is to connect you with your soul mate's energy so you can feel how they feel, enabling your subconscious to recognise them when you meet – maybe then you will take notice of them and let fate do her thing!

Do this exercise at a time when you are relaxed and feeling positive and open. Do not try too hard: simply let the images and feelings flow towards you. Of course, you can use The Gallery technique (see page 52) but what would be the fun in using the same method over and over? I like my clients and students to have fun, but also by learning different exercises, they work different visualisation muscles.

If you do this exercise at a time other than your bedtime it may be an idea to set an alarm clock for one hour's time – otherwise you may drift off to sleep and forget all the information.

◆ Begin with the Opening Up technique (see page 42).

◆ Imagine you are on board a huge cruise liner. You are standing on the deck as the ship leaves the port. The only difference between this cruise liner and any other is that this ship takes you into the future.

♦ Shut your eyes and imagine yourself going into your cabin and snuggle down. Know that in a short while you will relax and will feel as if you have been asleep, yet in fact only a few moments have passed. Relax and feel time passing now. Imagine you have opened your eyes and see your perfect soul mate. What does your partner look like? What colour hair and eyes do they have? Do they look like a peaceful person, or vibrant? Are they smiling? How do you feel with them? Happy? Relaxed? Comfortable? Secure? Do you feel happy?

♦ Soak in all the information so that you can discover all that you can about your future partner. Use all your senses – smell, taste, touch, sound and vision to collect the information you need.

♦ Now imagine it is later in the day and you are making a meal – it is your partner's favourite. Notice what you are making. Know that they will soon be walking through the front door. Feel the anticipation. Feel them walk through the door, walk up to you and kiss you hello.

Notice how good this feels. Now, this next part is very important. It will connect you and your partner, helping them to come into your life sooner.

♦ Feel your partner's energy, notice how they smell and feel, notice the warmth of your love. Now feel your energies blending. Keep that connection, and keep the blended energies as you make your left hand into a fist. Feel your partner's energy flow in your hand as you make a fist. You have now kept a little of that energy. Every time you want to connect with your future partner, all you need do is make a fist – and the connection will be made.

If you see someone you already know in your future vision, notice if the relationship is good or if there are difficulties. If the relationship you see if not going well, sink back into your cosy bed and ask to be shown an alternative future, a different life path, and one that would occur if you were not with this person. Snuggle down and imagine you are waking up with your love next to you.

I have had one client try four different life paths before she found the man of her dreams. She is now very happy and she confided, 'At least I do not have to take years to find the right one. I can try them out first with you.'

◆ Do the closing down technique (see page 44) to finish.

Will I be with my current partner in the future?

My years as a tarot consultant have taught me exactly what the public want to know about the most. Aside from finding 'the one,' the next question many people ask is, 'Will I be with my current partner in the future?'

You can use The Gallery exercise (see page 52) to find out if you will stay with the person you are with now and take the guesswork out of your future.

My client Peter came to me with this exact question. He told me that he felt he had wasted so much time on the wrong woman. He said, 'I put so much into the relationship and now I feel as if I have wasted the best years of my life. But now she is saying that she wants me back. I don't know what to do.'

Peter was distraught and confused. He felt he could not go through more heartbreak but he still loved her and wanted to give her a chance. We did The Gallery exercise to see if they had a future together, but in his future pictures Peter couldn't see his ex. He saw himself with a new girl and a child. They looked very happy.

Out of curiosity Peter looked at another picture with a clear question in his mind about what would happen to his now ex-girlfriend. He told me, 'How odd, I can see her with a friend of mine. He has a girlfriend, so I doubt that.'

Within a few days, Peter found out she had been secretly seeing his old friend and they were now together. The Gallery saved Peter from even more heartache.

Will I move on from my break-up?

I love the old saying, 'If only I knew then what I know now.' Most people wish they had hindsight, especially after a bomb-shell. Imagine being happily married for 20 years then your partner runs off with a traffic warden. Or, as the case with a number of my clients, their husband comes home one day to say, 'I'm leaving you for my secretary' and she's half his age! Believe me, in my job you see it all plus the devastation and the hard time the deserted have in moving on from the pain and rebuilding their lives. I've had big burly men over six feet tall crying in my office because they have lost the woman they love. Few things hurt more than to have the person you adore leave you for someone else. You sit and imagine them with their new lover, laughing together, looking into each others' eyes, visiting friends that were once your friends, eating meals together and making love. It's torture and truly soul-destroying. Only someone who has suffered this will know just how bad it feels.

Alice was a woman who really needed a boost. I knew that Future Life Progression could give her the injection of positivity she needed and help her overcome the pain of her break-up.

As a young woman she had given up a promising career to support her husband as he built his acting CV. She did everything she could to help his success. Alice desperately wanted children but her husband, Colin, had persuaded her to wait until he was rich enough to support them. By the time this happened – you couldn't switch on the TV without seeing Colin's face – it was too late. 'At least we have each other and everything we have worked for,' he told his wife.

Colin preferred to manage his own career but in truth it was Alice who did all the managing, unofficially and unpaid. She believed it didn't matter as long as they were progressing.

One night Colin finished his run in a successful show in the West End. He left a message on her mobile saying he had booked into a hotel near the theatre as it was late. Alice knew something wasn't right. She told me, 'I could feel it in my bones. There was something in his voice that shrieked guilt.' Alice knew where the rest of the cast often stayed and so she telephoned the hotel, asked for Colin and was put through to his room. You can probably guess the rest – a woman answered the phone. Alice drove the two-hour journey into town and found Colin with his co-star. He admitted they had fallen in love and he wanted to marry her.

When Alice came into my office she cried for 15 minutes

before she could utter a word. Then between sobs she said, 'I really don't know what you can do for me, but you've helped some of my friends for different things. In a nutshell, I have no career, all my friends are through Colin and he is parading his new girlfriend around. I have no life.'

Alice was so nervous I wasn't sure I would be able to work with her. She was also terrified that in 10 years' time her life would still be empty, but my instincts had told me this would not be the case. As I've said before, my intuition often gives me a snapshot of my client's future and I saw briefly that her future was rosy.

So, I took Alice forward five years using The Gallery (see page 52). The first thing she said as she looked at a picture of herself, which she saw as a huge photograph, was, 'Wow, I'm in good shape. I can see I've been working out, I never had time for myself when I was with Colin.' Then, I asked her to find the picture of her home and step inside. Alice went quiet and said, 'I'm living in the same house, but . . .

'What is it?' I asked her.

'I must be dreaming – there are three children with me. We're painting pictures at the kitchen table.' I asked her to see whose children they were. 'There is a man there they are his,' she replied.

'And who is he to you?'

'Oh, he is my husband. I have remarried, he has three lovely kids. They're like a ready-made family,' smiled Alice.

'What has happened to your ex?' I replied, intrigued. 'Find a picture that shows his life.'

'He's no longer with the girl he left me for, she's moved on to a more famous actor. He is looking quite old now and his career isn't going so well. I hope this isn't all wishful thinking.'

I reassured Alice that what she was experiencing would indeed happen. Afterwards she told me, 'I don't wish my ex any ill, but I do admit it does make me feel better to know they won't stay together. I don't know if any of this will come true, but at least it has given me some hope for myself.'

Alice called me two years later to tell me she had met a wonderful man with two children. She told me, 'Can you believe this? I'm pregnant even though I thought it was too late for me. When I told you that he had three children I was right – I just didn't realise one of them was with me.' I was delighted that she had finally found happiness.

It can take a long time to get over a break-up. It can feel as if our whole world has crumbled. But using The Gallery to see your romantic future can ease the pain and help you to move on.

Using Future Life Progression to Move On

◆ Have a clear question in your mind as you move along the tunnel, through the curtain and into the gallery. Focus on the future as you do this – you will not longer feel sad about the break-up, and you will also be moving on with your life.

◆ The key is to move forward until you have resolved the issue. By looking at specific time frames you could arrive at a time when you still have problems, but by allowing the session to be open-ended you will go to the exact point where you find your happier life and resolution. It is important to move to the point just beyond where you have moved on and found your new life. This will be a very empowering time for you and give you great encouragement right now.

◆ As you move towards the picture, know that you will see yourself once again happy and in love. Then as you step into the picture, feel those feelings. Focus on these positive emotions and draw them into you. By drawing in the fresh and happy energy you will help yourself move on to happier times and no longer be bothered by feelings of hurt and upset to do with your ex.

Bringing the Future to the Present

One of the biggest benefits of Future Life Progression is that you can link to the positive parts of your future self and bring these powerful connections back to your current self, your present time. This technique is especially helpful if you are suffering from pain following the break down of a relationship. You really can connect with your emotionally healed future and bring some of this strength back to your present time.

I know this works for a fact, because after hundreds of FLP sessions with clients I've discovered by moving someone beyond a problem to a better place it's quite hard for them to make the negative feelings come back.

The best way to understand this concept is to think of a time in your life when you've been stuck in a situation. Maybe you were floundering in a relationship that was going nowhere, yet you found it almost impossible to move on. Or remember how devastated you were when you split up with someone and thought you would never find love again – yet you did.

Now, imagine if your future self travelled back and showed

your current self how good you would feel when you moved on, and maybe met someone new and better.

Imagine if you could actually feel the emotions of your future self and future reality, in short, your future life choice, once you've taken that decision. I promise with this knowledge you will soon leave the dead-end situation behind and be keen to experience the better future you've glimpsed.

Several years ago I took part in the Wellbeing festival in Dubai. They never do anything by halves in this modern Arabian city, and so 66 mind, body and spirit experts were invited from all over the world to run workshops, teach and lecture. It was a massive event with well-known speakers such as Deepak Chopra and Paul McKenna.

I had three large workshops to conduct on Future Life Progression. At the time FLP was little known anywhere in the world, including The Emirates, but the response was wonderful – a mixture of fascination and 'how can we learn more?' Afterwards a shy lady came up to me and asked, 'Is there any way you can fit me in whilst you're here? I do realise you must be busy.' A haunted look in her eyes made me say yes. Somehow I knew she had been carrying a difficult problem for a long time.

In the session the next day, the shy lady, Cat, told me, 'I need to look into the future to see if I will ever get over my ex Michael. Thoughts of him plague my mind, yet we've been apart for five years.'

She was now in a new relationship with a wonderful new man called Shaun and felt that her past relationship with Michael was holding her back from moving on with her life. She told me, 'I love my fiancée so much – I just don't understand why I can't let go of my previous partner.'

I took Cat on guided visualisation using The Gallery (see page

52) and we jumped forward five years in time. She described her beautiful home and her wonderful lifestyle. Yet something didn't feel right to me so I asked, 'Are you happy?'

She replied, 'I feel nothing. I wish I hadn't married Shaun.'

'Do you still think about your ex Michael?'

She replied, 'All the time. But my husband is a good man.'

So five years into the future, she still hadn't moved on from her love affair with Michael. Cat's voice carried sadness and her sparkle had gone. My instincts told me to move her on quickly to the ten-year mark. I asked her to see the years passing by quickly as numbers in her mind.

As she arrived ten years from her current time she saw herself still married to Shaun, but now she had two children and wanted a divorce. At that point my instincts told me to take her forward yet another five years – sometimes we need to keep moving forward until we find the solution to our problem.

I could see an image of Cat glowing with happiness. Cat's face softened as she connected to this time and the bitter edge evaporated. Now when I asked her if she was happy she replied, 'I truly am.'

'What is happening in your life?' I asked.

'I am now married to a wonderful man. We're deeply in love. This is how it should be.'

'Do you ever think about your ex Michael who caused you all the pain and stopped you from moving on?'

She replied, 'Oh I have forgotten all about him.'

I asked Cat's current self to speak to her future self because our future selves give us the answers we need – and I cannot think of a better guide. (You will learn how to apply this skill in the next chapter, which focuses on utilising Future Life Progression to make good moves at work.) Cat's future self told her in these exact words, which she repeated out loud, 'Don't be with someone that you don't love. You need to know that your ex Michael wasn't as interested in you as you were in him. Therefore it was not meant to be.'

I brought Cat out of The Gallery and back to the present time and she said, 'This is weird, but I feel as if something has lifted. I've immediately just thought of Michael and I feel nothing. Our relationship all seems like such a long time ago and it has no impact on my life now.'

Just having this realisation allowed Cat to release her ex right there and then (because all thoughts contain energy). She cut the invisible bond that had tied her to him unnecessarily. Future Life Progression had helped her to find out what she needed to know and make immediate changes, beginning with a change in her awareness.

At the end of the session Cat told me, 'I can now see that our relationship wasn't the great romance that I thought it was, and just knowing this alone will allow me to move on.'

As she left I commented, 'If you were truly in love with your current partner, the feelings for your ex would have dissolved.'

Cat nodded her head and replied, 'I know.'

Later she sent me a text message saying, 'Anne, I don't know if I can ever thank you enough for this wonderful feeling. I know what I have to do.' She felt happy and had found a sense of inner calm even though she was facing the break-up of her current relationship with Shaun. But for me as a therapist, the most important aspect of her session was connecting her to all the powerful and positive energy she has in the future and bringing it back to her present time, her current self. Now she won't have to wait 15 years for all this to happen. In fact, I doubt she will have to wait more than three years for the love of her life to appear.

Choosing Between Two Lovers

If you don't have a problem finding love, or holding on to it, you may have too many choices! Partners can be like buses: there are none for ages, then several suitors arrive at the same time. To make the right choice, try the following exercise which I call The Elevator.

....

The Elevator

◆ Begin with the Opening Up technique (see page 42).

◆ Imagine yourself in a hotel lobby. In front of you is an elevator. Step inside the elevator and press the button that says 'one year'. If you want, you will be able to see other buttons that say 'five years', 'ten years,' or even six months, if this is the time frame you wish to work with at this present moment.

◆ As you press the button and begin to rise upwards you know that you are moving forward in time.

◆ The elevator stops and the door opens. You notice two doors in front of you. The door on the left has the name of the first person you need to know about. The right hand door has the name of the second person. (Do add more doors if you have more suitors – you lucky thing.)

◆ Open the door to the first room and step inside. Know that as you step inside you will feel just what it will feel like in the future if you choose this person. Imagine how life would be if you were with this person. Do you appear happy? Stressed? Relaxed? On edge? Do you and the person spend a lot of time together? If so, do you have fun?

Is there a balance in the relationship or is one of you doing all the taking and the other all the giving? Do you show respect for one another? Do you like doing the same things, or is one of you making a lot of compromises and spending a lot of time in the other's world? Focus on your physical relationship: do you match well? Has the relationship grown stronger as time has gone on or has it weakened and begun to fizzle out? Look at your day-to-day life with this person and see if that is the life you want to have.

◆ Once you have found out what you need to know, try the second room. Again, go through the same process. Look at the second person you need to know about, your possible partner. Look at the same areas as above and in as much detail.

◆ Make sure you go with your first impression. Do not try to 'make' yourself feel anything – simply allow the feelings to flow.

◆ Don't forget to carry out the Closing Down technique, as outlined on page 44, to complete the exercise.

Am I with a Commitment Phobic?

Looking at Lorraine you would think she didn't have a care in the world. Tall, slim and dressed in an expensive suit with a crisp white blouse, black high heels and immaculate hair, she appeared to be an icon of success and fashion. Lorraine jumped into my comfy chair with a grin and said, 'I need to know absolutely everything.' She had a list of questions but the main thing on her mind was love.

Lorraine had been in a relationship with a top Italian lawyer, Luigi, for eight years and, like many people, she wanted to know if the relationship was going anywhere. She told me, 'I need to know what the future holds for us. We live apart and neither of us wants to give up our independence, but this relationship doesn't seem to be progressing. As time goes on we seem to want different things out of life. I really need to know where I will be in five years' time.'

On the surface they seemed like the perfect couple. They were very touchy-feely, they did lots of things together and both of them lit up when the other entered the room. They liked the same food and the same music. So what was the problem?

Lorraine told me, 'I'm a few years older than Luigi and we've both realised that he wants to be married and have children. I can see sadness in his eyes when he sees other people with their children. If he had asked me in the early days of our relationship I would probably have had a child for him, but now my first grandchild is on the way. I have brought up four kids from a previous relationship, and the last thing I want now is another baby.'

She went on to explain that although she loved him dearly, Lorraine almost felt as if she should help him to find a wife. 'It must sound weird,' she said.

I asked her, 'So where does all this leave you?'

'Well, this is the difficult part. I just cannot imagine life without him. I feel as if I won't have a future if I walk away. I need to know if we will ever commit to one another properly.'

I took Lorraine five years into the future, again using The Gallery (see page 52), where she described living in a skyscraper in America. She saw a photo of the building, then jumped inside. 'It's all very high-tech. I love this place. I can see all over New York,' she told me. Lorraine described the apartment, 'It's huge but minimal. Everything is white except for the odd splash of black. The view is amazing, This is some place,' she told me.

I asked her to look around the apartment to see if there was a man living there with her. She glowed as she said, 'Hang on, I can see men's shoes. Hey, there is a man. He looks really nice; he's wearing a smart suit. I feel he is my partner.'

'What is his name?' I nudged her for information.

She replied without hesitation, 'Jack.'

'What does he look like?'

'He is dark and has a strong jaw. He has dark hair, he's big and broad and the opposite of Luigi.'

'How do you feel?' I said next.

'Really happy and contented. It's a lovely, easy relationship.'

'Do you still hear from Luigi?' I know she would want to know this so I asked for her.

'No. To be honest, I feel as if I have forgotten all about him.'

I then took Lorraine forward to see her life ten years from her current time and she told me, 'I can see mountains and tall trees. This is the most beautiful place.'

'Where is this?'

'I am in Canada, in fact we are in Canada. I'm still with Jack. I feel he is my soul mate.'

I then took her forward to her next lifetime. Her face flushed as she told me, 'I'm aboard a craft. A spacecraft. We're all in uniform.'

'So where do you live?' I said, thinking, this is fascinating.

'Aboard the craft. This is where we live.'

'Who is there with you?' Lorraine looked so happy as she said, 'Jack is here. He is my partner. He is the captain on the ship.'

'Is there anyone else there that you know?'

'Yes – Luigi. He is here too.'

'What does he mean to you now?'

'He is just there in the background. He is a lot older than me this time around. He looks out for me, like an uncle. Jack is my love. We're so connected.'

I asked her, 'What is the main thing you have learnt from this?'

She replied, 'I don't have to worry about being single if I leave Luigi. Love is always there for you. I know that now.'

Sometimes what we wish for is not the experience that will benefit us the most, and we can be blind as to what really is the right path for us. You may have even looked back yourself at troubling events in your life and later been thankful these occurred because they acted as a catalyst to push you in the right direction. It can be hard to move on from a difficult relationship but when life takes a new turn, after maybe you've gained the strength to move on and met someone new, you can look back and realise that the relationship was part of a bigger picture to bring you to where you are now.

Changing a dead-end relationship

Jayne seemed to have it all – a wealthy family, a jet-set lifestyle and the best money could buy. She also had her own successful design agency. Her friends thought she had a charmed life, but Jayne had one problem that plagued her day and night. She was tortured by an on-off relationship. Somehow every time things started going well, she and Tom had another huge row.

I soon realised she was used to getting just what she wanted when she wanted. She called me early one morning asking for an appointment that day and she was most put out when I said I was booked up.

'But I need to see you right now,' she said indignantly. I scheduled her for a few days later.

Jayne was nervous about having a session. She told me, 'I don't think I'm going to like what I see.' The tempestuous relationship was with a man who lived overseas so the busts-up were even harder to reconcile. They had finally split up three months before and she didn't expect to hear from him again. She told me, 'I just need to know if he will ever appear in my life again.'

Usually I take my clients at least five years into the future, as by going five years ahead most of the immediate questions will be answered. Jayne was adamant that she needed to go just one year ahead to see if he had popped up in her life, and as she was so firm about this I agreed to go along with her. It was obvious that Jayne was not ready to look deeper into her relationship and I never push my clients. They let me know what they need to find out and I work with them. At times I may try a gentle nudge, but it is up to them what they are ready to deal with. So I was surprised at how easily Jayne relaxed.

After a minute or so, Jayne said, 'I am in a ski resort with him. I hope I am not just imagining this.'

'Just go with it,' I told her.

Jayne then said, 'This is so odd. I can clearly see myself inside a log cabin in a ski resort, which is not that surprising because he often works as a ski instructor. But I can see myself cooking him breakfast while he reads the newspaper. I can see every detail of this room. There is a picture on the wall of a sunset; the sofa is cream-coloured with brown cushions. How very odd. I can even see that he's wearing a red fleece.'

Jayne dismissed the session telling me, 'Oh this is just my wishes coming into my head. It has been three months and I don't think I will see him ever again.'

I didn't expect to ever hear from Jayne because she was so dismissive and negative about her session. But 15 months later she came to see me and revealed, 'He called and said we should meet and talk.' Luckily I've a good memory so I knew exactly what she was talking about.

'We met in Austria,' she began. 'I arrived at midnight and he picked me up from the airport and drove me to the ski resort where he was working. We arrived in the early hours and just collapsed into bed, we were so tired. The next morning I got up, went downstairs and poured a coffee.' I knew what was coming next. She continued, 'I had this strange feeling but I couldn't work out what it was. I began cooking him breakfast – he has always loved bacon and eggs – and I realised that the feeling was déjà vu. Yet I'd never been to the resort before in my life. The room looked so familiar as he sat reading the newspaper. Then suddenly I realised he was wearing a red fleece, and the whole Future Life Progression session came flooding back into my mind. I really thought it was all nonsense but what I saw was in front of me that moment was the image I'd had in every detail. It was astonishing.'

I suggested to Jayne that it may be a good idea to look further into the future to see where they both were in a few years time. She declined. I knew Jayne wasn't ready to face those issues in her life, but that when she was I would be there to help her.

I would love this to have a happy ending but the last I heard the relationship was even worse and they were on the point of separating again. In a dead-end relationship people go round in circles – and it can last for years.

....

Revitalising a Dead-end Relationship

Again, you can use The Gallery (see page 52) to add zest to a relationship that has gone stale. (Don't forget to use the Opening Up and Closing Down techniques described on pages 42–44). You can ask questions such as:

◆ What has caused my relationship to break down?

◆ How can I revitalise my relationship?

◆ Is there some outside factor such as work or relatives that has caused a problem?

◆ Is there something I can do differently?

◆ Is this worth pursuing or is it time to move on?

◆ What is the most important thing for me to know about this issue?

This time as you move along the tunnel keep your questions clearly in mind. Be aware of your need to know what has caused the relationship to become dead end. As you move into the Gallery, be open-minded and aware. You need some answers and the picture you will see will provide it.

Sylvia used The Gallery for this very purpose. She needed to know why her marriage had become so flat and dull. She nervously looked into the picture then stepped inside and she saw that she was bogged down with her family and her husband had got into a rut of watching television whilst she rushed around trying to look after children, parents, sisters and their offspring.

Then Sylvia asked to be shown that if she let go of some of the family demands how things could be different. She immediately saw herself and her husband on holiday sipping cocktails. She told me, 'I can see that we have both aged ten years because of all the pressure, but in the second picture we looked younger and happier. In future, my family will have to look after themselves a little more. They won't like it, but that is how it must be. My doormat days are over.'

◆ Like Sylvia, focus on the first picture and find out what has created the flat feeling. Step into the picture and notice all the variables and how you have arrived at this point. Step out of that picture and now focus on the second picture, which will show you an alternative picture – how life can be different and how to achieve this, and bring you a happier and more positive life.

◆ What have you discovered in the second picture? Have you had a makeover? Taken time out for fun? Made more effort with your partner? Had a heart-to-heart chat? Moved house? Moved on from draining people?

- ◆ Stay as long as you wish and soak up the good feelings. This will help you to bring the more positive future into your life right now.

- ◆ Use the Closing Down technique to finish (see page 44).

Finding Out if your Partner will Ever Settle Down

Sometimes we just need some reassurance that our partner will turn into the person we know they can be! Tony wanted Future Life Progression to see if his girlfriend would settle down. He said, 'I really love her and want to marry her, but I'm holding back from proposing because she is quite a ladette. She goes out with her friends and gets so drunk she sometimes doesn't remember the night or the journey home. I'm a homely type of person and I want children, but this worries me. I don't want my kids having a drunken mother.'

In The Gallery (see page 52) Tony found a photograph of his wedding day and indeed he was marrying Denise. He had a tear in his eye as he said, 'She looks so beautiful.' Then he looked at little more serious as he said, 'There are two bridesmaids and they are both the ladettes she goes out with.'

I wanted to see how they were getting on so I asked him, 'Go forward a few months and see how married life is treating you.' Tony beamed as he said, 'She doesn't go out any more boozing and the two bridesmaids are both courting. In fact one of them met her boyfriend at the wedding – he is an old college friend of mine. Who would have thought?' he said wistfully as he told me about how the girls had all quietened down and how his old friend Johnnie and their bridesmaid Cherie often popped around for a cup of tea.

We then peeped a year ahead and Tony grinned as he told me, 'We're expecting our first child and I have to drag Denise out now. She has really settled into family life.' I didn't hear from Tony again for a while, but when I bumped into him in town one day he had a big grin on his face as he opened up his wallet to show me a picture of his daughter.

Using FLP to Help Overcome Grief

One of the most endearing cases I have ever worked on regarding love was with Rosemary, a delightful lady in her 50s. Rosemary told me that her beloved husband had passed away two years earlier and she was still grief-stricken. They had met when they were both 14 years old and had been married for over 30 years when he had a sudden heart attack and died. There was no warning and no preparation. They had spent a great deal of their time planning their retirement where they would do all the things they had no time to do now in their busy working lives. They had often joked about how they would be two old codgers together. She felt cheated.

She told me, 'I still feel as if he is going to walk through the door. I put a brave face on for my children. I don't want them to worry, but this is eating away at me.'

Rosemary had been to various mediums, some of whom had given her very encouraging messages from her husband. She had undergone grief counselling and her kids had sent her on the mandatory cruise, but still nothing seemed to ease the pain. The mother-of-four was a strong woman but she just could not let go.

She contacted me after reading about Past Life Regression and wondered if she and her husband had had past lives together – perhaps that would give her comfort? She was a very attractive lady and I felt she had a lot of life still to live. I felt that Future Life Progression might be better for her. I gently suggested, 'You know you're still young, and by looking forward into the future you may see some something that helps you to move on. There may be more happiness there than you can imagine.'

Rosemary reminded me of another client who had also lost her husband. She had been grief-stricken but had since remarried. At the time she would have responded angrily to any suggestion of remarrying, but as time moved on she met a lovely man. I felt that if Rosemary could see something in her future to give her hope she would let go of the grief. As Rosemary said herself, she could see no future but she wanted to find peace again, so she agreed readily to try FLP.

In The Gallery she found a snapshot of herself with her grandchildren when I took her to the five-year point. She was looking after them during the day whilst her daughter worked. Her daughter had always said she wouldn't have children, but Rosemary could see that she had changed her mind and she was blessed with three gorgeous little ones. Just this news made Rosemary smile, which was lovely as she had looked so broken when she had entered my office.

We moved forward again. At ten years, she excitedly told me, 'The children are much bigger now and doing well at school. They are lovely.'

She spoke so proudly about them that it was wonderful to hear. Remember, in her present time she had no grandchildren at all. Rosemary wasn't very interested in actually seeing a future lifetime, but instinctively I knew she should have a look at her next life. Rosemary was soon visualising and she told me about her life as a nurse.

She said, 'I love my job and feel it's a real calling.'

I asked her if there was anyone around her in that life that she knew in her current life. She replied, 'I have a husband – he is a doctor, we work together.'

I smiled as I asked her, 'Does he remind you of anyone you have known in your current lifetime?'

'There is something familiar about him. I feel I already know him. Oh – it's my husband! We will be together again.'

I could see the sadness lifting from Rosemary with this revelation. The grey tinges of grief in her aura, which had cloaked her body about half a metre out, were flushed away and a pinky-yellow appeared in its place. This new colour suggested happiness, as shown by the yellow, and pink is a classic colour for love.

Believe me, I had a big lump in my throat as I brought Rosemary back to the current point in time. Since then, I've had several people who have suffered the bereavement of their partner and to know they will be with their loved ones again in a future life gives them peace and hope.

Love can bring us the happiest and most devastating times of our lives. If Future Life Progression can help you just a tiny bit to achieve contentment in love, then I will be happy. Apart from love, work and your vocation in life is the next most important area to get right. The next chapter helps you do just that, because I'm going to teach you how to find your dream job and make the most of your current opportunities.

CHAPTER 4

How to Find the Perfect Job

How many people can truly say that they love their work? Can you imagine spending the best part of your life in a job that makes you miserable? Many people do – I regularly see clients who tell me that they are unhappy at work. The majority of this group tell me they just 'fell' into what they do, their families pushed them or they went into a profession because it was safe or well paid – little thought seems to have been given to enjoyment.

I've also found that if someone is in the wrong job they won't have a particularly good connection with their colleagues. But if you find a way to earn a living doing a job you love, you will discover that the connection and rapport with your work colleagues will be wonderful, and many may end up as lifelong friends.

Here's how I use Future Life Progression to find the most suitable vocation for my clients – one in which they will truly thrive and prosper.

The Six Outcomes

The following six themes crop up repeatedly in sessions with clients and during workshops. In this chapter, you will discover how you can use Future Life Progression to achieve the outcomes listed below. If you don't see your situation or goal on the list below, don't worry. By the end of the chapter you will feel confident enough to adapt the techniques to suit your specific situation.

1   Find career direction in your current job – make the right moves to maximise your potential and escape a dead-end role.

2   Walk a new career path – identify your true vocation and implement a career change with confidence and success.

3   Time-manage your working life better – sort out your work overload by prioritising what you need to focus on and what you can leave to sort itself out.

4   Build your confidence – Future Life Progression will show you how to follow your dream and make it come true.

5   Make changes in your life – if you're unhappy with your life path, Future Life Progression will help you to know that you *will* escape your rut.

6   Find fulfillment – put the fire back into your working soul.

I use the following exercise, The Doors, to pinpoint answers to your career questions. The process uses a time frame of five and ten years, in order to view the long-term outcomes of your actions. You will also be able to see your alternative futures and career options, enabling you to make the very best career moves. During the process you will see and feel just how each option could turn out – stopping you from wasting time on courses, jobs and companies that are not suitable.

As you work through The Doors, you may experience much more than you had expected. Just let this happen – allow all the available information to flow through you. By doing this, you may see future issues that you had not thought of or asked about, and be prepared when they happen. These are the unexpected events in life that cause us so many potential problems, from redundancy due to a company take-over to a colleague unfairly blaming you for something. As well as helping you avoid, or be one step ahead of, unexpected events, you also won't miss any golden opportunities.

....

The Doors

◆ Before you begin, do the Opening Up exercise, as outlined on page 42.

◆ Just imagine you are in the hallway of a grand old house, a beautiful stately home. Look around at all the splendour, the rich carpets and chandeliers. The sun streams in through the window.

◆ Walk over to the window and really get a sense of walking across the vast hallway. Now notice that the sun is shining in through some French windows. Just walk up and open the doors. As you step outside, you find yourself on a terrace. The air is so clean and with each breath that you take you relax more deeply.

◆ Look around the beautiful garden and notice how it has been so cared for. Notice that there are steps leading down from the terrace. Walk down the steps, and as you do this put aside all your current thoughts and feelings. Simply concentrate on what you need to know in order to progress your career. Put everything else aside as you focus totally on this one request. And go deep within yourself and find the answers that you need. Because deep inside you already have the knowledge. It is already within you, stored deep within you.

◆ Breathe the clean fresh air as you walk down the steps and enjoy a sense of peace and wellbeing. Look down and notice that there are ten steps – really look at them. A butterfly has landed on the third step. There is grass growing between some of the steps, and some of them are slightly cracked. But you know you are perfectly safe and have a sense of peace as you walk down the steps.

◆ At the bottom of the steps is a small courtyard and in the centre is a lawn with a bench. Sit down on the bench. In front of you is a wall with three doors. Each door represents a choice that you have. (If you have more or less than three choices, you can change the number of doors to fit your situation.)

◆ Think of your choices and notice that on each door is a sign with a word representing your choice. For instance, if you were choosing between a number of options you would have a door for each option and each door would bear a company name. Alternatively, the choice could be which university to go to or which subject to study.

◆ Now focus on the first door and walk towards it. Turn the handle and walk inside. Notice what you see inside. How does it feel? Do you feel happy? Do you feel you are progressing, or treading water? Do you feel you made the right choice, and that you are in the right place? Allow yourself time to really soak in just how you feel. Notice any details such as people you would be working or studying with. Stay as long as you wish and take in all the images and feelings that come to you.

When you have learnt all you need, leave the room. Close the door behind you then go back out into the courtyard and sit back on the bench. Take time to take in the atmosphere and how you feel.

◆ Now focus on the second door, then walk up to it and enter the room, just as before. Soak up the feelings and images. Does this feel like a good option? Do you have feelings of uncertainty? Do you connect with the people who are around you? Do you feel they support you, or are they aloof? Are you all on the same wavelength, or do you feel like the odd one out? This is often a good clue as to whether an option is right for you. Once you have gained all that you need, leave the room then again, go back into the courtyard and sit on the bench.

◆ Now focus on the third door. Again, walk inside and gain the knowledge that you need by asking questions as before, noting all your responses.

◆ Stop and imagine time passing quickly. Do you feel that a lot of progress is being made? Can you see how you will build on this option in the long-term future? In years to come, do you feel that you will be happy with this option?

◆ Once you have been through all the doors, sit back on the bench in the courtyard and review what you have discovered.

Stay a while and focus on what is the best way forward for you.

◆ Do the closing down exercise, as outlined on page 44, to finish.

Every time you repeat The Doors exercise either for love questions as in Chapter 4, or here for your career, you are entrenching it in you conscious and subconscious mind, creating an accessible 'door' to walk through whenever you need to. With practice, you will be able to use The Doors at will, whenever you need guidance. You will also find that the images you see and the information you get from them will flow more strongly.

Top tip

Remember, you can use The Doors exercise to help you pinpoint your best career moves, see if you are in the right place and doing the right things, or to see if there are better options available to you.

Finding Your Career Direction with Future Life Progression

Whenever I've heard horror stories about people making big mistakes concerning career moves, I wish I could have guided them with Future Life Progression. It's such a useful tool for giving insight into situations relating to work. Sometimes

people just need that little bit of help, even a snippet of information, to guide them toward making better decisions and even
avoiding ruin or tragedy.

One such client who needed such help was Suzanne. Her
opening words to me were, 'I need to find out about my job and
what my boss thinks of me. I've coasted along for two years and
don't feel like I'm getting anywhere.' Suzanne was doing
administrative and reception work for an estate agent. She had
been promised a lucrative post selling houses and earning
commission, but the sales job never materialised. She wanted to
know if she needed to move or stay with her current company.

I explained to Suzanne that I could take her forward five years
to see how things had panned out in her job, and I could also
take her forward ten years and even into a future lifetime if she
was interested. She replied, 'I only need to see five years into
the future. Crikey, I have enough to worry about with this life
let alone thinking about the next one.'

So using The Doors, Suzanne discovered her future at work. I
asked her to step through a door representing five years into the
future to find out if she should she stay with her current
company. She looked stunned. 'How cruel – they have had no
intention of promoting me at all. I can see them smiling to
themselves.'

'Why haven't they promoted you?' I asked.

'Because I am useful on the front desk, well spoken and I get
on with everyone. It is hard to find someone good who is efficient, and will work overtime without extra pay when
necessary, so they have deliberately held me back.' Suzanne
choked out the words.

'Oh I can't believe it,' she continued. 'The office junior, who
is with me now, has been promoted over me – and still they are

promising me more. They are telling me how they are going to open another branch and give me a key position, but the boss smirked as he walked away. I can't believe this, it's horrible.'

'Okay, let's imagine there is a door in front of you and this door leads you to an alternative future,' I suggested. 'One that will be your future if you change your direction now.'

Suzanne's shoulders relaxed and again she sighed, only this time it was a sigh of relief.

'Hey, I am working for their rival. He has offered me jobs in the past but I've been too loyal to take the opportunity. It seems I have learnt to look after myself for a change.'

'How is the job going?'

'Fantastic, I'm running a whole team, selling and training up new people. My new boss has put a lot of faith in me,' she beamed, 'and we are selling three times more houses than my old firm.'

As Suzanne gathered up her coat and bag to leave my office she looked determined and told me at the door, 'I'm now off to talk to my boss's rival about that job he keeps offering me.'

I bumped into Suzanne quite recently and everything she had seen was starting to come to fruition. She was happy and felt like she had direction and responsibility instead of being stuck, and held down, in a dead-end job.

Case study

Just recently Jenny came to see me. She had two strong job offers that were completely different. Both had great prospects and she was terrified of making the wrong move.

'Whichever I choose will take my career in a very definite, but different, direction. One will be more managerial so I could possibly work my way up the ladder. The other would be more academic, and so I could make a name for myself,' she explained.

Equally, both could turn out to be a waste of a good few years of her life with little chance of catching up on the other direction. As you can imagine, Jenny was losing sleep over this quandary. She used The Doors exercise (see page 85), and as she walked through the first door marked 'managerial', I asked her, 'What made you take this direction?'

'Everyone around me thought it was the best option. I was so confused I listened to them'

'Was it a good move?' I asked.

'No. I'm so unhappy. It is totally cut throat. I am just not the type of person to get ahead by being a back-stabber. I can see less talented people being promoted by stitching up their colleagues.'

I then told Jenny, 'Have a look at how your life would have been had you taken the other path through the second door.'

Jenny's face then changed completely; her features softened and her voice became sweeter. She told me, 'This is so wonderful! I have had papers published and I am working on my first book. But more importantly, I'm getting so much job satisfaction. I have set up a trust to help disadvantaged youngsters who would like to work in my field. One of my first, a young man called David, has just graduated I couldn't be more proud if he'd been my son.'

I could see tears in Jenny's eyes as I brought her back to her present time. Afterwards I asked her, 'So you know which decision to make?'

'Oh yes. Deep down the research option is what I would prefer but everyone keeps telling me how rich I would be if I take the managerial route. Now I can see it isn't what I want, and I will make more money on the academic route in the long-term anyway, by having papers and books published, and by becoming a leader in my field.'

Two years later, Jenny was firmly on course with a career she loved and was working on her first book. She glowed as she told me how Future Life Progression had saved her from a miserable working life.

Walking a New Career Path

As well as finding direction in their current job, many clients have found their true vocation with the help of a Future Life Progression session. I've had people go from being a photographer to an interior designer or bank clerk to an aromatherapist after a session with me.

Sally was a great example of a round peg in a square hole who was helped by FLP. She was forever being told off by her manager in the accountancy office where she worked. Sally like to chat and each day she would tell herself that she would concentrate and keep quiet, but somehow she found herself talking about everything and anything with her colleagues. Luckily, by looking at her future options she saw that she was much more suited to a job in selling. Her salary has doubled and her new boss says, 'No wonder she sells so much – she can talk for England!'

Clients also report back to me that after their initial Future Life Progression session they now make better decisions about their career. They feel more 'ready' to take a leap and take a risk – except it's not into the unknown as they have already seen the right future and direction to go in! If you think about it, by having a little taster of the more successful you, wouldn't you be encouraged to go for it? If you could actually feel what it's like to be 'top of your game' your doubts would leave you, you would become more self-assured and become aware of your real capabilities. Future Life Progression gives you this experience and clears the way of fear – one of the main barriers to success.

'The greatest barrier to success is the fear of failure.'

Sven Goran Eriksson

After trying various methods, I've found that the best way to find someone's true vocation is using The Crystal Tower visualisation. In this exercise, you connect with your future self and find out about your career and your options. This technique is also ideal if you have already decided on a chosen career but need to see how your present path will progress, you will want to know if you are moving in the right direction. Perhaps you need to specialise, or maybe your current department is not ideal for you? Here's how to find out.

....

The Crystal Tower

◆ Begin with the Opening Up technique (see page 42).

◆ Lie down or sit, whichever feels more natural for you. Now, I want you to imagine yourself walking outside in nature. It's a beautiful day as you wander along a winding path. You take your time as you slowly meander along, enjoying the peace and quiet of a lovely day. Lost in thought, you look up and see a tall crystal tower in the distance. It glistens in the sunlight as you begin to hurry towards it.

◆ As you arrive at the foot of the crystal tower, feel a sense of anticipation, wondering what is inside.

◆ Enter the building. Inside, it's even more beautiful. Everything is made of crystal as sunlight shines through the clear crystal roof and hundreds of prisms light up the foyer.

◆ Suddenly, you notice a kindly old gentleman who ushers you forward towards a steep escalator that ascends high into the building. You gaze up the escalator and see that it reaches a floor way above you. The old gentleman tells you that the escalator will take you to your own future career in five years' time and show you what options you have.

◆ Step onto the escalator and climb higher and higher into the air. You look down and know that you are leaving your present time behind. You climb higher and higher until you reach the top and step forward onto the top and only floor.

◆ This floor is pure crystal and circular with doors all around. Somehow you know that the door in front of you is your most likely future – the future that will happen if you stay with your present choices and stay on your present path.

♦ Open the door and step into a big white circular room. Look up and notice that images are beginning to flash across the wall. They flash across so fast you can't quite make them out. But soon the images start to slow down. Gradually, begin to make out images of your own life five years in the future. This is your future if you stay on your current path. What is happening with your work? Where are you employed? Who are you working with? Are you pleased with how things have turned out? Are you disappointed? Do you feel you could have achieved more? Or have you have done better than you expected?

♦ Notice if there are any areas that need improving. Perhaps you feel you should have studied more. Do you feel you have regrets?

♦ Once you have the information you need, walk back out of the room and into the hallway where you notice the other doors. They are marked with numbers that relate to your alternative life options. Look at the next door, numbered two, and walk though it.

♦ Don't worry if you wish to see all the options before making any decisions. You can pop through the other doors after-wards.

♦ As you walk inside the room, again you notice images quickly flickering across the wall. Gradually, they slow down. These images show you an alternative future – one that will occur if you make the necessary changes in your life right now. Know that you will be shown an alternative future that is achievable.

◆ Now focus on the future you, and in your mind ask your future self if he or she has any advice. The future you has the benefit of hindsight and has wisdom to impart. Take whatever answers come back to you, and know that you have the power now to make any changes you feel are necessary in order to give you the best possible future.

◆ Finish with the closing down technique (see page 44).

....

By looking five years into the future, you can usually find out what line of work you will most be suited to. Then by moving forward to the ten-year point, you can see how that career progresses and grows. Often, I see the development stage at five years and then the peak or near-peak at ten years. A client of mine, Lucy, is a short but sweet example of how to use the five- and ten-year mark to help make career choices. Lucy was about to take a course in psychology and she wanted to see if it was the right move for her. She moved forward five years and indeed saw herself with a successful practice, but by the ten year point she had written a book and become quite an authority on the subject.

Another strong example of how Future Life Progression and The Crystal Tower can help you find your true vocation is Pete's story. He wanted a new career, but he found it difficult to talk about his feelings about work – and although he was very unhappy, he also felt guilty and ungrateful.

Pete had been in IT for 20 years. He said, 'Where I came from it was unheard of for any of us to go to university. Most of my school mates went into the local factory but my dad was a mechanic and ran a garage and did okay. He and my mum scrimped and scraped for me and my brother to go to uni.

'I don't know what is wrong with me,' he confided. 'I've had all the breaks but I hate my job, a 16-year-old could do it. Now it's too late to change.'

Pete was convinced that being in his 40s meant it was no use trying to start a new career. 'People don't want you once you are past a certain age,' he told me. 'I'm now on antidepressants I'm so fed up. I've worked at the same place for ten years but have no friends in the company.'

Pete was saying something I had heard many times from my clients when they had come for tarot readings. Employers seemed to only want younger people to fill their vacancies. It's awful to say that many people feel washed up at 40, even though they've experience and talent. I hoped that Pete would find some happiness in his future, which is why I suggested a session of Future Life Progression.

At the beginning of the session, Pete told me he could never imagine moving out of London because 'that was where all the work is'. Fortunately for him, things looked very different in five years' time – after he jumped forward using The Crystal Tower. I guided him through the process, and this is what he told me.

'I am living in the countryside in a little village. It's gorgeous; I never thought I would leave London. I didn't think I would like living out of town but I feel so happy here,' he said as he glimpsed his future self.

'What are you doing for work?' I asked him.

'This is really strange, but I am working with my hands and I love it. I also love village life and getting on well with the community.'

'What work are you doing with your hands?' I nudged him.

'I am restoring furniture. It is quite basic work but really enjoyable. I have also made loads of friends through this job.'

Pete told me he was living in a little cottage and although he had made more friends in the two years he'd lived there he was still single. As he arrived at ten years into his future, Pete was still in his little village and very happy.

'I am still working with my hands but I have developed my craft. I am more confident with it. At first I did the basic easy stuff, but now I am working on some major projects.'

I said, 'Ask the future you what advice has he has for you.'

'Get the ball rolling now,' Pete replied. 'Learn something to do with restoration. Don't worry about making mistakes – you can be too cautious. Nothing will change if you don't change it. You could still be in IT in ten years.'

'It's a scary thought that I'll still be in the same job in ten years', Pete remarked. 'And it does seem odd to be taking advice from my future self.'

As Pete went to the next stage, and slipped into his future life-time, I thought he had gone back to a past life as he began talking about working in a castle. But as he described arriving in some sort of vehicle which hovered over the ground it was obvious he'd travelled a long way forward.

'The people here are so pleased to see me. They are deter-mined to keep their history alive. I have specialised skills that can restore the castle and help to preserve it. I feel so happy, I can't think of a better job,' he remarked.

Pete did go on to train in restoration and eventually set up his own business. I know too that he will also find himself working in that castle in his next life.

Time-manage Your Working Life

People think of time management as 'What do I have to do today?' but actually that's short-term time management. Long-term time management is essential too, and it's critically important at work in helping you make the right moves. By having a strategy for long-term management you can focus your time and energy on activities that will pay off. For example, say you are a solicitor and you want to progress up the corporate ladder. Should you focus your energies on conveyancing (buying and selling property) or litigation? You could use Future Life Progression to find out which will be your strongest area. You might be a journalist torn between reporting hard news or writing features for the women's pages. If so, you can use Future Life Progression to explore different outcomes and plan your career, and time, accordingly.

Using Future Life Progression as a long-term management tool means you can develop your career and avoid wasting time learning unnecessary skills. How many times have you invested in a career, only to find it didn't work out? Or maybe studied skills or subjects that since became obsolete? Making these kinds of decisions about your career direction can be torturous. Future Life Progression can help you plan and use your time to maximum effect.

In the next exercise, Time Management Future Life Progression, you will find out how to put into place long-term career management. This is not about job moves, but acquiring skills in your current profession.

....

Time Management Future Life Progression

◆ Begin with the Opening Up exercise on page 42.

◆ Find yourself a comfy place to relax. Close your eyes and allow your breathing to deepen.

◆ Concentrate on your breathing and imagine you are walking up some stairs to a small building. Walk up to the top of the stairs and find yourself before the front door. Open the door and step inside.

◆ Walk right past a small reception area, waving 'hello' to the young receptionist. At the far end of the reception area there is a big blue door. Walk up to the door and notice it has your name on it. Reach out and turn the handle. Open the door and step inside.

◆ You are inside a small, cosy office. Look around and see that everything is laid out perfectly. The office has a warm blue carpet that is soft beneath your feet. In front of you is large dark wooden desk with a telephone, a notepad and pen, and an in-tray.

◆ In one corner is a large round lamp sending a golden glow around the room. In another corner is a water cooler with several cups.

◆ Walk over to the desk and sit down. Notice that the desk has three drawers.

    The top drawer has the word 'study' on it.

    The middle drawer has the word 'unexpected' on it.

    The bottom drawer has the words 'extra suggestions' on it.

Inside each drawer is a folder containing information that will guide you in your career and allow you to maximise your time. In a moment you will open each drawer, take out the folder and see what is inside. The folder will contain a suggestion or piece of advice for you. This may take the form of a word, a picture or even a symbol.

◆ Open the top drawer, marked 'study'. Reach in and take out the folder, and know that the folder will contain a message for you to develop your skills. It may suggest learning something or tell you which areas you need to read up on. Once you have received your message, put the folder back and close the drawer.

◆ Now open the middle drawer, marked 'unexpected'. Take out the folder and know that inside will be a message. This message will warn you of anything that you have not thought of or unexpected that could affect your career. It may warn you of an adversary or maybe a mentor. It could alert you to an unexpected opportunity or to something going suddenly wrong. This folder is very important because it can save you from a catastrophe or show you a major career break. Again, the message may take any form such as a word, picture or symbol. Once you have received your message, put the folder back and close the drawer.

◆ Now look at the bottom drawer, marked 'extra suggestions'. This folder will contain any extra advice that will give you the edge. This folder will contain suggestions that are less tangible, such as becoming more confident or dressing differently. Once you have received your message, again put the folder back and close the drawer.

♦ Take a few moments to review what you have learnt. The information you have gained from this exercise will enable you to fast-track your career. It will give you the edge and help you use your time wisely.

♦ Don't forget to carry out the Closing Down exercise, as outlined on page 44, to finish.

....

Building Your Confidence

Future Life Progression can show you how to follow your dreams. Apart from taking the wrong course in your work life, sometimes things happen that leave little option but to take a career break. For women, having babies probably puts more careers on hold than anything else. It can be gruelling stepping back into a professional persona, and regaining your confidence at work, after spending your days playing with Plasticine™ with a small person!

Charlene was a classic example of a woman who had put her career on hold for her little ones. When she came into my office she seemed rather shy and lacking in confidence as she told me her dreams.

She had always wanted to travel the world and have a career, but while she was still young her children had come along. Now she felt that her ambitions would never be realised. All her life she had dreamt of travelling across Africa and visiting Australia and the Amazon rain forests. She'd planned to study hard, gain some qualifications then go travelling. Her partner, Dick, shared the same dream. When they first met their conversations had been full of plans – in fact, this was what drew them together; they felt they had so much in common. Now it all seemed very far away as they were bogged down with nappies and bills.

She told me, 'I love my little ones. I really wouldn't be without them. But now I do sometimes wonder if I will ever do anything exciting with my life.'

As she arrived five years into the future, using The Crystal Tower (see page 94), Charlene saw herself walking into a college carrying a pile of books. 'Are you studying?' I asked her.

'Yes, I am studying psychology and training to be a counsellor.'

'How is it going?'

'Very well – so far I have passed all my exams.'

I was curious to find out how Charlene had managed to take the course. In her current time she was struggling as a full-time mum to two young children and she couldn't afford course fees and child care. By finding out how she'd managed to overcome these barriers it would greatly help her in her current life, not just by letting her know that a better life was to come, but also by finding out just what she needed to know to progress.

Charlene told me, 'I took an evening course in child psychology and found I had a real knack. My tutor recommended me for a grant and scholarship, which I succeeded in getting. My mother retired and so was able to look after the children and my partner was given a promotion, so he is earning a lot more.

She continued smiling, as she reviewed her life five years into the future, 'I feel so confident and self-assured. It is odd to think I was working in a dead-end job and felt quite useless. Now I have other students looking up to me and asking me for advice.'

Finding her talents and discovering how to get things moving not only benefited Charlene, but the many people she will go on to help. She told me, 'I am so happy to know I will do something with my brain. I thought it was too late for me.'

I then asked her about travel. She said, 'We take a lot of long holidays with the children so we are getting to see different places. I am not too worried; I know that I will get to travel when the children are older.'

People who grow a great deal in their current lifetime have often achieved even more in their future lifetime, and this was the case with Charlene. When I moved her forward to the ten-year mark she told me, 'I'm holding a briefcase and wearing a smart pin stripe suit. I'm a lawyer. Gosh, I seem so in control and confident. I discovered in my current lifetime that I could achieve a great deal by studying. This pushed me forward in this lifetime, where I studied even harder and achieved even more and although it is a different field, I use my skills to help people.'

After the session Charlene told me, 'This has really pointed me in the right direction. I missed university and thought I wouldn't get another chance, but now I can see that I get to study – and in more than one lifetime.'

Charlene looked quite different as she left my office. There was a new cool and calm air about her as if a little bit of her confident future self had stayed with her. Charlene now knew she would make a success of her life, and she was ready to take steps towards it.

Tips for Building Your Confidence with Future Life Progression

Each time you tap into the future, using The Doors or The Crystal Tower, and you reach the point where you have met your goal, notice how your future self is full of confidence – just as you would be when on the right path.

Remember, you may have to walk through a few doors, using The Doors, or visit The Crystal Tower, to find how you can reach this point – but you will find the answer of how to achieve your dream. And every time you make contact with your future self using these two methods (The Doors and The Crystal Tower), take a few moments to connect and soak up the positive feelings. This will help build your confidence and by actually 'feeling' yourself using your future ability you will feel more confident about making moves towards it.

Making Changes in Your Life

Unhappy with your life path? Future Life Progression will help you find the road to escape your rut. Many people have a Future Life Progression session because their life is not the way they want it, but making change isn't easy. In fact, most people are imprisoned on a hamster wheel of paying bills and surviving. It's hard to follow your dreams when you have food to put on the table. Elaine was no different except that she was very successful in the corporate world, but despite being financially secure she somehow never felt satisfied and could see no way out.

Elaine was living in an industrial town just outside London and commuted into the city each day. She had an impressive salary but it just didn't feel right. Elaine wanted to be doing something that made a difference. She told me, 'I simply cannot afford to just pack up and play with something else. I'm stuck here for a very long time yet.'

The last thing Elaine expected was to see herself living her dreams and looking out to sea, but at the five-year point in her session with me Elaine said, 'This is so completely odd. I am living by the sea and I am known locally for helping others. People come to me for healing and other treatments. I am often called upon for advice. How can this be so? It must be a fantasy.'

Like most people, Elaine thought that her future vision must be her imagination – it's hard for most people to see any real change in their lives unless the path is already there. I prompted her to keep looking and asked, 'Where do you live?'

'It's a gorgeous little house,' she enthused. 'But how can I ever afford to leave my well-paid job? How will I survive?'

Elaine had been divorced for some time and had had her fingers burnt in previous failed relationships so I was keen to ask her the important question. I'd a feeling the answer would be a happy one. I inquired, 'Does anyone live there with you?'

'Yes a man, a professor. He travels a lot and there are children in the background. Older children.'

'Are they his children?'

'Yes, and I can sense a baby. I think I am pregnant. I don't know why, but I feel it is a boy.'

At the time Elaine had no idea how she would meet a professor. It's often the way that when we look into the future we cannot see how we will end up in certain circumstances. Imagine if you'd had Future Life Progression ten years ago. Has life turned out exactly how you expected? Most people would be amazed at just how much their lives had changed for the better in that space of time.

Two years after the progression Elaine contacted me and said, 'Anne, you will never believe what has happened. An elderly relative passed away and left me a cottage by the coast. I didn't even know this place existed. I'm now living there and it's wonderful. And this you really will never believe – I was offered a job by a university a few miles from the cottage. They asked me if I would like to join them even though I lived so far away near London. At the time, they had no idea I was moving up the road from them. I now have a new job at the university where I'm doing something really useful, head of a team of PAs to lecturers, and I have the time and space to develop my healing skills. The universe works in mysterious ways.'

A year ago Elaine sent me a message to say, 'The progression was three years ago and now my life is very different to how I was living before. People come to see me for healing and treatments and I'm surrounded by academics. The future man isn't in position yet, but I still have a couple of years for him to turn up!'

Elaine sounded so happy and I couldn't have been be more pleased to have been able to use Future Life Progression to help another one of my clients find their true path in life.

Get Yourself a Goal

It's important to decide exactly where you want to go job-wise, otherwise you will have a vague attitude towards your career – 'I just want to have a happy work life' or 'I just want a better job.' This approach may seem okay, but by not identifying what you want you will lack direction and will find yourself stuck in a job with no future, or have other people deciding your career path. But by defining what you want, you can then work towards getting it. You will have a goal.

◆ Rate your current work life out of ten, with 10 being perfect and 0 being dreadful.

Job satisfaction (   )

Rapport with colleagues (   )

Progress and promotion prospects (   )

Learning (   )

Growing as a person (   )

◆ Now imagine you are in the same job in ten years' time. What is your immediate feeling – are you pleased? Do you feel sick at the thought of working with the same people? Are you disappointed by your lack of progress? I have asked these types of question many times, and in every case my client's face has dropped at the thought of doing the same job in the same way that far into the future.

◆ As you focus on this thought and notice your reaction, stop and think about your ideal scenario. How would you like things to be? What would you like to be doing to earn a living and where?

◆ Now stop again and notice how you feel. Are you positive? Happy when you think of your ideal situation? This tells you that you want to make progress and where you should be going in your life job-wise.

◆ Now notice your main worry when you project yourself into the future in your current job. To project yourself into the future, choose the exercise most appropriate to your needs. To find your ideal job, go to The Crystal Tower (see page 94). If you need to weigh up your options in your current post use The Doors (page 85), and if you need to know how to use your time and efforts wisely, use the Time Management exercise (page 100).

Find fulfilment: Re-light the Fire of your Working Soul

The people who seem to have everything are envied by many, but often they are deeply unhappy and have no idea why. The rich and famous can spend a fortune on therapy and still be none the wiser about the dissatisfaction in their lives. As you have seen illustrated in the stories so far, Future Life Progression can often unlock the information that will lead to a more fulfilling life.

Carl is a good example of this dilemma. He's a hugely successful television scriptwriter, and at any one moment there will be something of his currently on the screen or about to appear. His work includes a wide variety of children's programmes, period dramas and a high-action cop series.

When he came to see me he said, 'I should be a happy man but I feel nothing, I'm just so unfulfilled I just don't understand it. Most people would give their eye teeth to have work like mine. I make lots of money and have a brilliant job, yet somehow I always feel that something is missing.'

Carl had initially wanted Past Life Regression but had since heard about my work with Future Life Progression and asked if he could also have this in the same session. He was keen for me to work with him, but also said, 'I'm worried that you won't be able to relax me. I question everything and I'm not a good subject.'

'Great,' I thought, 'He doesn't want much.' I told him that it depended on how good a subject he was as to how much I could do with him. I also explained that is was up to him how much he relaxed and how he needed to work with me to get the results.

I took Carl back into a past life where he immediately saw himself in a war zone. He was a very young man, maybe 17 years old, and he had lied about his age to fight for his country. Back home it had seemed like an exciting idea, but now weeks of trenches and seeing people around him die had given him another reality. He had the optimism of youth and had a cocky air in his voice as he described loading up a big gun. Then suddenly a shocked look appeared on his face and he said, 'Oh, I have been shot.' He died at that tender age, stunned to have done so. He felt he was invincible and had tragically found that he was as mortal as everyone else.

He immediately went to another past life that appeared to be downtown Chicago in the Depression era. He was a runner for gangsters, and again very young and very cocky. He had money in his pocket at a time when few people did, and again he felt invincible. Carl saw himself leaving a building after collecting some money, then suddenly saw himself lying on the ground in a pool of blood.

He said, 'Crikey, this doesn't look good for me in my present life. I hope this doesn't mean I will die young in this life too.'

In both his previous lives he hadn't lived beyond the age of 20. In his current life he was nearly 40, and so I told him he had gone way beyond the age of his previous deaths. Besides, it doesn't follow that he would die young again in his current lifetime. Out of interest I asked him if he'd had any near-misses in his youth. He replied matter-of-factly, 'Oh yes, I shouldn't be here now.' He didn't elaborate and I didn't push him. I then asked him to ask his higher self why he survived this time and he was told, 'You have important work to do.' He then gave a cynical 'Yeah, right.'

Now it was time to look at where he was heading. I took him forward five years using The Crystal Tower (see page 94) and he saw himself in America driving a huge car. He said, 'This can't be right. I would never drive a car like that. It's so tacky.'

I told him I felt that the car and the house had been arranged by people he was working for, a large multinational company. I could also see he was now in films. Carl had the same image but still he had the flat feeling about his work. It looked as if he had just arrived in America. I took him forward another five years and there he saw himself in a huge house, this time in a style he liked. He was obviously hugely successful and enjoying his work a little more, but still felt as if there was something missing, something that he just couldn't identify.

It was time to take him forward to a future lifetime and for someone who thought he would not be a good subject, he was proving to be very interesting. I could hardly wait to see what and where he would be.

'This can't be right,' he said. 'I am standing on a balcony preaching. There are lots of people below. I would never preach. I hate religion.'

I replied, 'Go and listen and find out what you are saying to the people.'

He said, 'Oh, I am telling them not to listen to governments or religions but to listen to themselves. I am helping them to find their own inner voice and inner wisdom.'

He face softened. He had found inner fulfillment and contentment. I said, 'So what is the lesson for you now in your current life?'

He replied, 'To use the power of my words to influence people in a positive way. To really help people and write things that will encourage them to be more themselves. Hey, this is amazing, I have the key to making my job enjoyable and worthwhile.'

Very often people find their true life purpose through Future Life Progression. And as they do so they immediately look lighter and more at peace, as did Carl. I then instructed him to talk to the future him and ask if there was anything he should be doing now.

His future self told him, and he repeated it aloud, 'You write for kids and can really steer them in a positive direction and give them great inner strength. You can influence youngsters to lead a good life.'

The last I heard of Carl he was working on a script that contained an important message. The script would become a film with a feel-good factor that showed people how their actions affected not only their own life, but the lives of others.

Just think that when you discover the perfect job for you, your true vocation, how much happier you will be and in turn how you will help to make the world a better place. In Chapter 7 you will discover how to find your soul's purpose, but if you are struggling to find out what type of work you would be suited to, try the following exercise.

Childhood Dreams

◆ Do the Opening Up exercise, as outlined on page 42, before
you begin.

◆ Find yourself a comfy place to relax. Clear your mind and think
back to your childhood. What games did you play? What was
your favourite television programme or book? What did you
pretend to be? What did your family say about you?

Did they ever say:

'She loves animals'

'He is like a little monkey, he climbs so well.'

'Suzy has a wonderful imagination.'

'Billy loves tearing around on his bike.'

◆ Make a note of all the answers and within them will be clues
to your ideal job. The boy who whizzed around on his bike
would make a great driver; the girl who loved animals would
be the perfect vet or veterinary nurse. The little girl who
pretended to be Alice in Wonderland would make a great
writer or actress.

◆ What were your childhood dreams? Take a moment to
connect – it may give you clues to your current lack of career
fulfilment.

◆ Don't forget to carry out the Closing Down exercise, as
outlined on page 44, to finish.

Your True Vocation Is Waiting For You

Spend time on the exercises in this chapter. By finding your true vocation you will greatly enhance your life, and even if you are already in your perfect career you will gain insight into how to be more effective, gaining more from your time and input.

When you find your true vocation you will work well and be efficient and enthusiastic. You will apply yourself more. Food seems to taste so much better when cooked by a happy chef. An angry or upset chef can give people tummy ache. Can you imagine buying clothes woven by someone who loved their work? They appreciated the softness of the yarn and they took great pride in the design. Later, seeing someone wearing something made with their cloth would make them beam with pride. Now imagine wearing something made in a sweatshop by people being exploited. You can 'feel' the difference.

I have seen so many people make lifelong friends through their work, yet this rarely happens if you are in the wrong place doing work you dislike. Take time to find the right work for you, and it will affect your life for the better in many ways.

Given the amount of time we spend at work it is a dreadful waste for so many people to be dragging themselves off to something that makes them miserable. I believe that if more people loved their work, the world would be a much happier place.

The world is changing fast, and you need to know if your work and your industry are going to change, or if there will be new developments that may suit you. Future Life Progression can alert you to great opportunities. For example, if you see that a rival company is about to start trading, you could get ahead and be first to market your new product, be it a type of bra or bread. In fact, whether you are an inventor, a business owner, or simply someone who wants to progress in a particular field, the next chapter on Seeing the Potential at Work will help you discover what lies ahead, giving you inside information and the edge over your competitors – be they individuals or global companies.

CHAPTER 5
Seeing the Potential at Work

In this chapter you will discover how Future Life Progression can help you get the edge in business, and generate new, relevant ideas and products. Innovative ideas make a company stand out ahead of the competition. Market leaders in all industries, from music to engineering, spot the zeitgeist before everyone else.

Learn how to use FLP to maximise your business success (or enhance your role if you're employed by a company) in the following areas:

- Spotting future trends – discover how a product is selling in the future

- Finding solutions for business problems – and make the right choice of business partner

- Managing your finances – how to play the stock market

- Identifying a hot property – find the next property hotspot at home and abroad

- Creativity – how to jump into the future to generate ideas

Spotting Future Trends

Can you imagine burning the midnight oil to get your grades to go to university? Then, after working hard to get a degree, discover that your chosen field of work has dried up and you are unable to get a job? I have seen this happen time and again. Many people make the mistake of thinking that the world will never change, or they believe that something will always be in demand. A good example is the career rush in the 1980s when many people dashed off to train in IT, and at first some did earn piles of money. But as the 90s ticked on, IT stalled and the run-of-the-mill IT 'experts' faced redundancy, or earned half their previous salary and were left struggling to pay their high mortgages. I know this is true because I met many of these individuals when they came to me as new clients looking for help with their career direction.

My message to you is that the world will keep on changing and you need to know what will be the next big thing. You also need to know what will peak and die out very quickly and what is worth a long-term view. Trends occur in any field of work. I remember years ago when I asked my optician about contact lenses (yes, it was a very long time ago!) he looked at me and said, 'They will never catch on. Besides, you are far better off with glasses.' He retired shortly afterwards.

Even for people working in the New Age field there are trends. In my Nan's day, reading tea leaves was very popular; now it's rare to come across anyone with this skill. In the 60s there were also far more palmists. In the 80s lots of people became aromatherapists, and today there are many Reiki practitioners. For the last five or six years angels have become all the rage. Have angels suddenly decided to pop up among us more often, or is it fashionable? If you spend a fortune to become one sort of a therapist and, within a year there are hundreds of other people all clutching the same certificate, you could find that you have wasted your money.

Luckily, by working with my clients I often gain an insight into future trends. If several people mention green hair will be 'bang on trend' (as the glossy magazines say) then I know what to advise my clients in hair and beauty. Often clients just want to know that things will work out okay, or they simply have a question or decision to make. Yet during the session they discover a wealth of information that will put them streets ahead of the competition.

By the time beautician Cosima came for her Future Life Progression session, she was thoroughly fed up. She had just endured the worst Christmas of her life and wanted to see if it would get any better in the future.

'I've not enjoyed my last couple of Christmases. My boyfriend and I haven't had any money, and we have had to rely on other people's hospitality. I love visiting family but I do dream of having Christmas at home and being able to repay everyone who has looked after us.'

She also dreamt of having her own salon and making Christmas special for the staff and customers – something salons she had worked for had not done in the past. I took her into the future using a method I call The Trend Spotting Café (see page 120). At the five-year point, Cosima said, 'Oh, this is odd. I am at my uncle's salon. It looks different. It is lilac and very upmarket. Wow, it's mine now. I must have bought it from him.'

I asked her about her staff. 'I have three girls working for me. I visit it every day to make sure it is in order.'

She continued, 'Downstairs the salon is really funky with nail bars. Everyone looks in as they walk by because it looks such fun, but upstairs is so special, like a sacred place. I can see flickering – oh, it's candles. People arrive upstairs then take their shoes off. I do not allow shoes,' she said firmly. 'They get changed into a robe. It's neutral décor with amazing lighting.'

I asked her what treatments she offered. 'All of them, but especially anti-ageing. I am using a computer – it is something really new. I am not sure how it works but it helps with anti-ageing. This is cutting edge stuff. The wrinkles are on the computer screen and we watch them plumping out. None of this is out now, but when it is I will know to offer this to my clients. This will be the biggest thing in beauty on the high street and I will be first in the queue.'

Cosima went on to describe products that were fruit and vegetable based and completely natural.

At ten years into the future, Cosima seemed a lot firmer in her speech, both business-like and confident. 'I have three salons and I am just arriving at a big house. I think it is a hotel. I am not sure what I am doing there.'

I asked Cosima to move forward to see what the purpose of her visit was. 'I am holding a meeting. I have my own product range and I am talking to my reps. I pop into my salons to see how they are doing and I promote my own products. They are very good. I am very proud of them'

'And your home life?' I ask.

'I have a large detached house and three children. There are two boys and a girl – they are running and playing. We have everyone over to us each Christmas. The whole family comes over.'

Knowing how big Italian families can get I said, 'That must be a lot of work.'

'It is wonderful and worth everything,' Cosima enthused. 'I have all this because I knew exactly what to invest in. In the beauty business you can waste so much money on something that looks like the next big thing and simply doesn't take off'.

Recently Cosima dropped by to tell me she was off to view a property which might be suitable for her first beauty salon. We both know it will be the first of many premises.

How to Spot Trends

No matter what you do you, whether you are a beautician like Cosima, or a property developer, you will need to know about upcoming trends in your field. I've developed the Trend-spotting Café so you can use this version of the process to hook into the 'zeitgeist' in your field. The more you practice this visualisation the more accurate and detailed information you will be able to bring back from the future to the present moment.

....

The Trend-spotting Café

Find yourself a comfy place to relax, take the phone off the hook.

◆ Begin with the Opening Up technique, as outlined on page 42.

◆ Let go of all your thoughts and worries. Leave your current day behind you and imagine that you are sitting in a coffee shop.

♦ Take time to build up the picture of the café. Around you is a wide range of people sipping their lattes and cappuccinos. There are a couple of young mums chatting and a businessman in a pin-striped suit reading the *Financial Times*. A lady solicitor reads a glossy magazine, and there is a young man who has just started his first job.

♦ Notice there is a large digital clock above the heads of the staff that displays the day, month, year, hour and minute. As you look at the clock, notice the dials begin to spin. You notice that the days are passing like minutes as the dials spin faster and faster.

Eventually they slow down and reach the usual second by second movement.

♦ Look around the coffee shop. Notice what the people are talking about. What are the young mums, whose children are now much bigger, talking about as they sip their coffees? Lean in and concentrate. Are they talking about the latest music? What clothes and hair are in fashion? What TV programmes and films are now highly rated?

♦ Now focus on the businessman. He has an eye for good investments. What is selling like hot cakes? What has boomed recently?

♦ Now focus on the lady solicitor. She is hard-working and very spiritual. What gadgets have made her life easier? What new spiritual trends is she reading about in her glossy magazine?

♦ And now look at the young man. He has now been promoted

and is working his way up in his company. Which cars are selling well and which does he dream of owning? What are young men of his age spending their hard-earned money on?

♦ You can place your own characters in the coffee shop and discover trends in any areas you wish, especially in your own field – just zone in and concentrate your whole session on that person who will give you your answers.

♦ Carry out the Closing Down exercise (see page 44) to finish.

How to Market-research a Product

You can use the following quick exercise, Product Testing, to 'test' how well your own product will sell. This product can be anything from coffee in your café to engine parts!.

Product Testing

♦ Use the Opening Up technique, as outlined on page 42, to begin.

♦ Imagine where your product would be sold – perhaps a shop, a bar or internet site.

♦ Now see yourself at this location. If it is a shop, imagine that you are standing behind the counter watching customers walk in. Notice how they respond, what they buy and if the shopkeeper looks pleased with sales. If it is an internet site, imagine watching the orders arrive by email. Notice if there is a steady flow or just one now and again. Stop and see if this feels profitable.

◆ My clients have used this technique for anything from a market stall to a restaurant. Even a high-tech software company actually saw their products being returned because they had a problem. They checked and found this to be the case, which saved them from upsetting valued customers.

◆ Carry out the Closing Down technique (see page 44), to finish.

....

Most people do stick to their own interests, products or field of knowledge when they use FLP for trend-spotting, so that they can hone and develop their skills. If you find yourself peeking into too many different things it may water down the profits. As in any business the rule is, 'Stick to what you know'. This really means don't scatter your energy, just concentrate fully on one thing. Now this is good advice, but in using FLP for business you may come across something new and exciting that is worth following up. If this is the case, explore the options and outcomes using FLP *and* the other usual business methods, such as market research, before making your final decision.

Finding Solutions to Business Problems

A new business can be a minefield. Far more companies fail than succeed. Business partnerships can be a major problem –

many people start a business with a relative or their best friend only to fall out. Yet when I warn them they rarely listen. A typical response will be, 'George and I have been friends since childhood and we have never had a cross word.' Or, 'I trust my sister-in-law with my life.' The whole scenario often reminds me of bands that start out so well then split up because of 'artistic differences'. As they're so successful, you would think that they would stick together and work things out, but their differences pull them apart.

Case Study

Jim, a garage owner, was one such case. He had recently gone into business with a friend but found the hours too long and decided that he wanted to sell up and emigrate to Australia. After six months, he suggested putting the garage on the market, but his new business partner persuaded him to not sell the business 'just yet'. After a year of waiting, Jim became frustrated by the delays and wondered if he would ever achieve his dream. His daughter had used FLP to see where she was heading career-wise, and suggested Jim do the same.

When Jim had his FLP session, using The Cosmic Laptop technique (see page 126) he was horrified by what he saw in his future. Things had gone horribly wrong. He visibly shook as he described how his business partner had pushed him out of the company and embezzled him. As Jim went into the future he gasped and said, 'I can't believe this. I'm so poor and I'm quite ill from the stress. We are still in England and we are on the bread line. How can that be?'

I asked Jim to work backwards to see how things had deterio-rated so badly. He said, 'I must be way off course but I can see my partner taking over the business and taking all the money. His girlfriend and her son seem to be in league with him. This is awful. I can't believe he would do this to me.'

Jim left the session refusing to believe it. He had known his partner for 20 years as friends and they had been in business together for around 18 months. Jim told me later that he didn't really believe what he had seen, but he could not shake off the images and feelings that he had experienced. He found himself constantly thinking about his FLP session and, as a result, a few weeks later he popped in to see me.

Jim revealed that just a week after the session, his business partner had brought his girlfriend into the company as a book keeper. He had told Jim that she was studying accounts and could handle that side of things to take the pressure off them. Alarm bells began to ring and then the girlfriend's son also joined the company as a would-be director!

Jim told me, 'I really don't know who else to talk to about this. If I tell anyone I know that I saw this in a FLP session they will think I am potty. Besides, everyone loves my business partner, so no one will believe me.'

Jim still had doubts that there was a secret agenda and so I suggested he got someone in to look over the books. 'That's a good idea,' he agreed. 'My brother-in-law is an accountant. Everything is kept at the garage – I will ask him over on Sunday to have a look.'

Thing were worse than Jim had thought. Already money had been moved out of the company accounts and his signature had been forged on some paperwork transferring money. Jim now knew for sure that the wheels were in motion for a disastrous future – unless he took action. Jim confronted his business partner and told him he had enough evidence to call the police. They agreed to sell the business, which they did for a decent price and in time for Jim to get out with some cash. 'My life would have been ruined if I hadn't had the FLP session. I saw the future, I didn't like what I saw and so I changed it. I dread to think how my life would have panned out if I hadn't have been given this forewarning.' Jim later achieved his dream of emigrating to Australia.

If you are thinking of starting a business or working with a friend, colleague or anyone in general, the following exercise will be useful and could save you a lot of anguish later.

The Cosmic Laptop

Find yourself a comfy place to relax, turn off your phone and clear your mind.

◆ Carry out the Opening Up technique, as outlined on page 42, to begin.

◆ Focus only on your business and what you would like to achieve.

◆ Allow your breathing to deepen and feel yourself becoming heavier and more relaxed with each breath that you take.

Breathe in and hold the breath for a count of three, then breathe out for three. Repeat three times.

◆ Now imagine you have a silver laptop computer in front of you, a very special laptop. Open it up and turn on the computer by pressing a button on the top right-hand corner. Watch the screen come alive. On the screen is an image of the person you plan to go into business with.

◆ In the bottom of the screen is a box. Type in the box the number of years you wish to look at, for instance five years. As you press the 'enter' key the screen flickers, then shows you and your business in five years' time.

◆ What do you see? Is your partner still around you?

◆ If not, what has happened? Allow the information to flow freely.

◆ If they are sill there, are you both working well together?

◆ Have they pulled their weight in the business?

◆ On reflection, was it a good idea to work with this person?

◆ Have you any regrets?

◆ Is there anything you would do differently?

◆ With hindsight, is there someone else you would have preferred to work with?

◆ Now ask the future business 'you' for any advice they have regarding this matter.

◆ When you have discovered all you need to know, reach out and shut down the computer, knowing that you can make more informed choices and move forward with confidence.

◆ Don't forget to use the Closing Down technique, as outlined
   on page 44, to finish.

....

Clients have travelled long distances to see me for help with
business problems, for which I'm flattered and grateful, but
when John called from his New York office and begged an emer-
gency appointment I was surprised. He added, 'Only you can
help me, please can you find me a slot?'

Luckily, a client had cancelled due to illness and I had a free
slot in a couple of day's time. John made the appointment and
flew to London the next day. He is very well known, startlingly
good-looking and so used to being recognised that he shielded
his face as he jumped out of the taxi outside my office. He has
a hugely successful television show, a chain of restaurants and
night clubs and a high-profile marriage. This chap seemed to
have it all.

John explained that he had a number of problems in his life
that he needed to resolve, and that he had heard about my work
from a top Hollywood actor. He said, 'If he says that you're the
best then you must be. You put his career and marriage on track
and you can do the same for me.'

I was flattered by his confidence and hoped I could help him
in at least one area of his life. As he told me his history, his voice
was flat and sad. I remember thinking, 'If someone could over-
hear the conversation they would think this fellow had nothing
going for him.' He was very low and very worried.

His marriage had hit the rocks and his wife was now openly
dating someone right under his nose, with the affair hitting
the gossip pages every day. The business and his television
show had been badly affected. In John's words, 'You can't

slump for long and get away with it in television. The competition is hot these days.'

To add to his woes, a rival had been making calls to various authorities implying restaurant premises were unclean and that he was evading tax. So now he was right in the middle of a stressful tax investigation. No wonder the man felt so down. I took him forward five years and he could see his business had changed somewhat.

John said, 'I have a TV production company and a night club. I've sold a couple of slow-moving restaurants and not before time. They were using up all my energy and causing me so many headaches. I am just starting another new venture again, I am not sure what it is but it is looking very good. Wait a minute – I can see a hotel. This is great.'

During the session, using the technique I call The Train (see page 130), we were able to pinpoint the resort area for his new hotel (later it thrived) and the best location for his night club. I also asked him about his love life and he simply said, 'I feel single.'

As we arrived at the ten-year point I could feel John had moved on a great deal. He said, 'I am wealthy beyond belief. I would never have expected this. I am living in a stunning house with a beautiful wife.' Now bearing in mind that although he had a great many problems to deal with and he was at a very low ebb, he amazed me when afterwards he said, 'I'm very relieved to see all this because I thought I would end up destitute. I'm uneducated and I thought I would never be able to get a job.' As he said these words his voice became very sad and quiet, and he continued, 'When I left school I was turned down for a job as street cleaner. If I muck up now I will never be able to get a job.'

Now this chap is a multi-millionaire – a household name with several businesses – yet he was worried he would not be able to get a very mundane job. He was actually worried that he could lose everything and end up penniless. He still had the emotional bruise from that early rejection. I just said to him, 'Hey, it might have been worse – you might have got that job as a street cleaner.' If it wasn't for the early rejection that had fuelled his passion to succeed, he may well have still been there.

The Train

Find yourself a comfy place to relax and sink into the chair or bed.

♦ Carry out the Opening Up technique, as outlined on page 42, to begin.

♦ Allow your mind to relax and as you let go of all thoughts other than the business dilemma you wish to resolve. Let anything other than this dilemma float away.

♦ Now relax your arms and legs and let your breathing deepen. Feel your feet relaxing and allow that sensation to flow up and into your legs and over your thighs and hips. Relax as the soft feeling of calm flows into your abdomen then up into your chest.

♦ Drop your shoulders as you feel them relax. Let the feeling of relaxation flow into your neck, softening all the ligaments and muscles.

♦ Feel the relaxation flow into your head, softening your facial muscles around your mouth and eyes, and moving right to the top of your head, again relaxing and softening. Now feel the relaxation calm your mind. As you breathe gently, feel a sense of peace flow over you.

◆ Now imagine you are walking into a train station. This is the smallest train station you have ever seen. As you walk up to the ticket office you see an elderly gentleman behind the counter. He smiles, and instead of asking you where you would like to go, he asks, 'What would you like to know?'

◆ Reply by telling him what dilemma you need to resolve. The gentleman hands you a first-class ticket and points you towards the platform. Notice that the platform is very small and it is the only platform in the station. You wonder how the station manages with just one platform for outward and inward journeys. Then you realise that the track is circular and runs around a large park. You can see several other stations dotted around the track.

◆ Now you see a sign above your head saying, 'You Are Here Right Now.' You then hear a train coming along the track and you notice a single carriage of a very plush train coming towards you. It stops and the same elderly gentleman opens the door for you, shows you to your seat and blows the whistle.

He explains to you that each station is an option. Soon you will be arriving at your first station. You realise that there is exactly the same number of stations as you have options – *plus one extra*.

◆ The train begins to slow down and you arrive at the first station. The elderly gentleman opens the door and you step onto the platform. You are immediately aware of how things will be if you take your first option. Soak up all the information you need. Notice how things will be financially and emotionally for you. Does this feel like a good option?

When you have all the information, step back onto the train and sink back into your seat as the elderly chap once again blows the whistle. As you trundle along the track, think about what you have just experienced.

◆ Notice the train once again slowing down as you arrive at the next destination and another option. Again step off the train and onto the platform and experience how things will be if you take that option. Take as long as you need. The train is your personal first-class carriage. There are no other passengers. Your train will wait for you.

◆ When you are ready, get back on the train and proceed to as many options as you need to arrive at the final station. This is your wild card, which provides a new option you had not thought of. Step off the train and experience this option. Does it feel like a good move or a bad one? Has it given you any new ideas or angles on your dilemma?

◆ Again, stay as long as you need. As you once again trundle along the track, completing a full circle, weigh up all you have seen. When you arrive back at the original station, decide which option is the best, the strongest and the most valuable.

Thank the elderly gentleman and take three deep breaths, in and out, in and out, and in and out. Now you are back in the here-and-now.

◆ Carry out the Closing Down technique, as outlined on page 44, to finish.

Managing your Finances

Aside from spotting future trends and overcoming problems, a stable business is maintained by sound investments and solid finance. But you don't have to own a multinational corporation to win at the investment game – FLP can give you the edge and ensure you minimise mistakes.

If you are in any doubt about how bad investments can impact on lives, think back to Black Monday in America on 2 May 1982, when oil prices crashed, and Black Wednesday in the UK, 16 September 1992, when the value of the pound plummeted. In both cases, city traders threw themselves from their office buildings. If you can remember the news stories you will have a good idea of just how someone can be ruined when their investments go wrong. But Future Life Progression can minimise the risks, and I believe that knowing where and when to invest must be one of its greatest applications.

The stock market is like playing a game of snakes and ladders. Stocks can rapidly slide for no apparent reason and panic can grip the trading floor – setting up a chain reaction. Afterwards, a big slide might be traced back to just one rumour, but in the chaos it is possible to lose everything. You can climb up the ladders and make a fortune – if you play well.

Stock market trader Greg Secker is always open to new ideas. Greg began his career at an early age. At 24 he was made the youngest ever vice-president of head of online trading for Mellon Capital Corporation in the United States. In 1997, he was responsible for creating one of the first global online dealing businesses supporting a money-market business that turned over billions on a daily basis. His training company,

Knowledge to Action Ltd, is the only one of its kind to be approved by the Financial Services Authority (FSA). He is the only trader to publish his dealings and results weekly online.

One of the reasons Greg has the edge over the competition is because he is open to new methods and ideas, among which he has experimented with Future Life Progression. In a recent experimental session of FLP with world-renowned hypnotist Paul McKenna, Greg was able to predict the following week's stock market results with 100 per cent accuracy.

FLP is still in its infancy and we are experimenting all the time but if this is anything to go by you could be using these skills and methods to make your life not only easier, but a lot richer, too.

I have noticed over the last few years far more people dabbling in the stock market. In the past it was the domain of the very rich and those in the know, but today there are books and courses on the subject, and anyone wishing to risk a few thousand pounds can dabble. If you are interested in the stock market the following exercise is worth practising. I am not telling you to gamble the farm, but to gently build your stock by dipping into the future and gaining a little inside information. The following exercise is the one Greg used to achieve his amazing result.

Disclaimer!

As with all the exercises in this book, they are carried out at your own risk. My advice is to play the stock market first using imaginary money. This way you will be able to see if you are hooking in properly and with accuracy. If not, you need to hone your technique further before parting with your real cash.

FLP Financial Forecasting

Before you play the stock market with Future Life Progression there are a few pointers from Paul McKenna I would like to mention. Paul told me, 'I find that many people don't achieve the wealth they desire because of two major blocks. These blocks are fear and greed. It's important for people to clear these barriers, otherwise they will find they will keep getting so far then reverting back to their original financial state of little or no money.'

Paul teaches how to clear these blocks in his book *I Can Make You Rich*. Paul also told me that with investments and the stock market there are so many variables that the success rate will be higher if you keep it simple and do not try to look too far into the future. As with many areas of FLP, we are still fine-tuning these techniques and so we would love to hear your results. So far we have found greater success by focusing on one or two companies and finding out whether their shares will rise or fall rather than trying to see a specific sum. You will have greater success by watching the trends and anticipating them. The next technique is based on one in *I Can Make You Rich* – try it and see what happens.

◆ Find yourself a comfy place to relax, turn off your telephone and sink into the bed or chair.

◆ Carry out the Opening Up technique, as outlined on page 42, to begin. Allow your breathing to deepen, feeling your abdomen rise and fall with each breath.

◆ Notice a sense of peace around you as your body relaxes

more deeply with each breath that you take. Concentrate fully on your breathing and feel yourself sinking into the bed or chair as your relax more and more.

◆ Now focus on what you need to know. Focus on the company whose performance you need to know about. Will their shares rise or fall? Are they good to invest in or is it time to sell?

◆ Imagine you have floated forward two weeks in time. You are looking at a newspaper dated two weeks from your current time. Flick open the pages and imagine in that newspaper is a feature about the very company you need to know about. What does the feature say? Has the company done well? Are they in trouble? Is there a takeover bid? Or new developments? Focus on the newspaper piece and either read or feel what it says.

◆ Notice any feelings you have about the company and the feature. Do you feel anxious? Nervous? Excited? Worried? Allow any feelings, good or bad, to float away into the distance. Do this for as long as it takes. By removing the emotions you will gain far greater results.

◆ After the emotions attached to the outcome have gone, go back to the newspaper feature. Are there any changes? How can you best utilise the information you now have?

◆ Once you have gained all the information you can, put down the newspaper and float gently back to your waking state. Absorb the knowledge you have been given and know that whenever you wish you can come back and look at another company or even monitor one particular company over time.

◆ Carry out the Closing Down technique, as outlined on page 44, to finish.

....

Remember this exercise needs to be practised, like all the techniques in the book, to give strong results. As you progress, you may even be able to read the headline on the newspaper story or pick up important key words. If this is the case, what does the headline say? If you can see it clearly, can you sense the gist?

Apart from the stock market all business and investments are governed by timing. What will ruin you one year could make you a fortune the next. As J. Paul Getty, the world's richest individual at the time of his death in 1976, said, 'Timing is not one of the important elements of successful investing; it is the most important factor. There are good and bad times to buy all investments. The key is to buy value when few other people want to buy.'

Property Matters

For most people, the greatest investment they will ever make will be their home. But whether you see yourself as a property magnet, or just want a cottage to call your own, you simply cannot afford to get it wrong. Clients come to see me with a wide range of queries, but without a doubt property is in the top five most stressful problems to battle with in your daily life. So much can go wrong, for example finding a huge problem with a property that will cost you a fortune to put right (even after a survey), like Philip who bought his dream home only to discover later that the foundations were unstable. The whole house needed underpinning and his life savings went on the repairs just as he was planning to retire. A little forewarning could have saved him so much anguish.

Some unlucky people bought property in areas that flooded, making them virtually uninsurable. Think back over the years about areas that once thrived but are now ghost towns. Mining villages have for generations kept families in good stead, but when the mines closed there was no other means of employment – and the village lost its lifeline.

Many towns are fed by just one or a handful of industries. A giant car factory decides to relocate where labour is cheaper, and the whole town is scratching around trying to earn a crust. You need to know where this might happen – to be forewarned can stop you making costly mistakes.

Case Study

As Kim walked into my office she burst out crying. It was five minutes before she could tell me her story. Like many people today, Kim had emigrated, moving to Spain with her husband, Dave, after finding their dream home. 'It was the perfect place,' she recalled. 'We had a large piece of land and even had our own orange grove. We spent a fortune doing up our villa. We spent our last penny, but it was worth it – or so we thought.'

Kim believed that someone was playing a joke on them when they received notice saying that a new road would run through their land and that they would have to pay for it.

'It actually ran right up to our door which meant losing our entire back garden. I spoke to the local authority who said they were about to build 500 houses next to us. Our quiet little home was about to be ruined. Then they told us that the road would benefit us and so we had to pay for it. And to top it all, they told us they were taking most of our land with no compensation.'

We looked forward in time, using the Magic Carpet Ride exercise (page 143) and saw that Kim managed to sell her property and move away. She told me,' I wouldn't want to live there now anyway but I am glad to see we are not stuck there.'

We moved forward a little further in time to see that Kim and Dave had moved back to England. She said, 'I feel such a fool. I have come home with my tail between my legs my dreams ruined.' My instincts told me that this was not the end of the story so I took Kim forward five years from her present time, where she saw herself in Portugal.

'I am so happy, this is actually better than where I was before.' We move forward ten and 15 years from her present time to make sure there were no further hiccups. From what we could see, Kim and Dave really did live happily ever after in their perfect home.

All many of us need is a break to get us going and with property so expensive in Britain, many find investing overseas their only option. The trouble is, this can be a minefield at times – trying to do business in a country in which you don't speak the language, plus the rules and regulations are quite different and can be exasperating. At times it can appear as if the local authorities move the goal posts just for fun, and finding the right help with builders, solicitors and surveyors is yet another problem. Even so, overseas property investment can be very lucrative.

My intuition has served me well over the years in all areas of my life including property, so when I had a dream of owning a flat on an odd-shaped island I took note. I had no idea where the island was or if it even existed, and at the time it was probably just a doodle on the back of an envelope. But as a psychic I take note of my dreams, so to double-check the information I took myself forward in time, using the Magic Carpet Ride technique on page 143, and again saw a series of buildings on an island in the desert. When I heard rumours of an island being built on the coastline of Dubai in the shape of a palm tree eight months later, I knew my island had appeared.

I scraped the money together to put a large deposit on a one-bedroomed apartment and within two years I had doubled my money. If I had not had the vision of Palm Island I would not have invested there and been rewarded with a healthy return. I truly believe my intuition, and Future Life Progression gave me the best possible investment opportunity at that time for my wallet and circumstances.

I told the story of Palm Island to Sharon, a client who was concerned her husband was about to make a bad investment. Sharon had attended several of my workshops on intuition. Her instincts were telling her something was not quite right with her husband's plans. Bill had been left £30,000 by his mother after her death and he wanted to do something constructive with it. They had worked hard for little return all their lives, now Bill believed he had the chance to gain some passive income and build some capital for their future.

I asked Sharon to relay the story to her husband whom, she informed me, would scoff at the idea, but I sometimes find people are more open-minded than their friends and partners realise. Two days later, he came to see me. A number of companies had cropped up, selling plots of land in the UK that would later be sold on to developers. By buying the land you became a middle man, earning a profit when it was sold on. The companies boasted that they had inside information on which land to purchase and which would get planning permission, making developers desperate to buy it. Several firms had indeed given their investors good returns. Bill told me, 'Sharon is convinced that land-buying is a bad idea. I have checked this firm out and they look good. They have plenty of assets and their past investors have done well.'

I asked Bill, 'Supposing this doesn't look good. What will you do?'

'I will check out some other companies, and if they are not looking good I will put the money in the bank for a while.'

The land company had told Bill he could expect a good return in three to five years. I took Bill forward to the three-year point to see if things had started to move. I asked him how the firm was doing, 'Um – that's weird. They are not here,' he said.

'What do you mean?' I asked.

'They have gone, long gone. I don't understand.'

'OK. Feel yourself move back in time until the point at which they went. What happened?'

Bill was silent for a few moments then he said, 'They made some bad investments I didn't realise that if they went down they took my money with them. This is terrible.'

'Now from your vantage point what would have been a better choice?'

'One of the other companies has thrived. They were my second choice to invest with. I can see they have made wiser decisions.'

Bill invested his money with the second company. It will

be a few years before he knows how much return he has generated, but he sleeps better at night knowing that the money is safe, and at least this company will still be around to pay him his dividend.

Finding the Next Property Hot Spot

Josh and Sarah also had a little money but they wanted to invest abroad, to speculate in Eastern Europe where properties could be picked up for a song. All they wanted to know was which country would have the next property boom. They asked me if they could have a joint session, that is for them to go forward together to see if they would find the same place. I am always up for an experiment, so I agreed.

They were a happy-go-lucky couple, giggling as I took them forward, but once I had taken them a couple of years into the future they became deadly serious. They wanted answers and were very focused about finding the right property to invest in abroad.

'Scan Eastern Europe and see where you are drawn to,' I told them. They both connected to Bulgaria, a place that has often come up in my own visions as booming in the future.

Next I said, 'Now scan Bulgaria. Which area are you drawn to?'

'Banks something!' said Sarah. Then added, 'I don't know this place.'

Josh said, 'I got something similar; it begins with a B, that's for sure.'

'What draws you to it?' I asked.

Sarah replied, 'I can see lots of people travelling there. Ah, this is a good sign. I can see a new airport and cheap flights from England.'

'What about you Josh, what are you picking up?'

'This is a sure thing. There is a Starbucks, so we cannot lose!'

Later that same week Sarah called and told me they had looked at a map and found the place, which was called Bansko. The couple had already arranged a trip to view some off-plan properties. On their visit, they heard that a new airport is to be built at Bansko and there are some new developments appearing around the area – so it looks like their FLP session gave them a hot property tip.

As any good property developer knows, a new delicatessen, mini supermarket like Tesco Express, a Starbucks and skips in the streets are sure signs that a town, or area, is on the way up. But by using FLP you don't have to wait for the signs to show the market is moving – you can get a foothold on the property ladder before the developers!

In the next exercise, you will learn how to use FLP to find your own property hot spot. Remember, you can adapt this exercise to suit your needs and location.

....

Magic Carpet Ride

Find yourself a comfy place to relax and just allow your mind to flow easily and comfortably.

◆ Begin with the Opening Up technique, as outlined on page 42.

◆ As you sink into the chair or bed, imagine you are sinking into a soft comfortable magic carpet that is floating just a few inches from the ground. This is the softest carpet in the world. Feel yourself totally sinking into the carpet and relaxing.

◆ The magic carpet moulds itself to your shape. Feel yourself floating gently as the carpet floats a few inches from the ground, just like floating on a boat on the river, gently, gently relaxing more and more.

◆ The carpet is so beautiful, made from the softest and purest silk. And just notice its colours – rich reds and blues, soft yellows and greens. See how this carpet is woven into the most wonderful patterns.

◆ Feel the carpet floating up and up into the air, higher and higher. You feel safe and loved as you float over and above houses, fields and roads. Look down and see a church spire and a long and winding river. Floating high above the trees and among the clouds, it is a perfect day, warm and peaceful. As the carpet moves slightly faster, you feel a cool and comfortable breeze.

◆ Now look down below and notice the richness of the fields. Just see below a rich green field and now a golden field. Now you are flying over a lake. It is the most beautiful blue lake you have ever seen; see the tiny boats and children playing around the shores.

◆ The magic carpet is now carrying you upwards. You are floating higher and higher over houses and towns and countryside, higher until you are looking down and viewing the entire country or continent you need to know about.

◆ As you float above the area, feel yourself hovering and looking down. Notice the area you are drawn to and as you become aware of it, your magic carpet sweeps down and allows you to view your chosen country or continent. What is happening there? Are there new developments? Does the area look as if it is booming? Or is it slumping? Can you see activity? Do you feel this is an area you need to invest in?

◆ Finish with the Closing Down technique, as outlined on page 44.

The Magic Carpet can take you to a foreign country or closer to home. It can find you the best street to buy in near your current location – or the best investment for you thousands of miles away. Where do you want your magic carpet to take you, home or abroad? Sit back and dream and think 'home' or 'abroad', then direct it to various other places like, 'near my current location' or 'somewhere near to me but more rural'. The combinations are endless and the technique can be adapted as you wish.

Creativity

Just imagine being able to look ahead to see what picture you have painted, house you have designed or hear a song you have written. In fact, I took one client, a female songwriter, forward in time to hear the result of her own creativity – which had yet to happen.

Vera had experienced some minor success. Several of her

songs had been used by singers just starting out, but none had been the hit she had hoped for and her big break as a songwriter had eluded her. She contacted me asking, 'Could it be possible with this future thing you do to see if I ever have a hit?'

'Better than that,' I told her, 'we can find out what it is called and how it sounds.'

At the five-year point she was still struggling along, but at ten years she told me, 'I have had several big hits.'

'The first big hit – what is it called?'

'*Forever and Tomorrow.*'

'Imagine it's playing on the radio. Can you hear it?'

'Yes I can,' she said.

'Listen to your hit song being played on the radio,' I suggested. 'Listen carefully and remember as much of it as you can. Let me know when you have heard it all.'

After a few minutes she said, 'That's it, the song has finished now.'

'Will you be able to remember it all?' I asked.

'Yes; I will start to write it up as soon as I get home. '

She couldn't wait to get out of the office and work on her hit single. With FLP you can reach your potential in the blink of an eye. Her song is now written and she is doing the rounds with it. But as she said herself, 'I know someone will take it up because I heard it on the radio in my FLP session.'

Discover your own Inner Genius

We all have hidden talents, but how many people discover them then put them to good use? You have talents, but what are they and how can you utilise them? Maybe you could invent something or write a chart-topping song? You may have an idea for a book or movie. Or perhaps you have the creative mind of an entrepreneur. Focus on the exact questions you need answering, then do the following exercise.

Thinking Out of the Box

◆ Carry out the Opening Up technique, as outlined on page 42 to begin.

◆ Imagine you're out in nature; it's a sunny day with a cool breeze. Visualise yourself sitting down to relax and feel at peace with the world. Look up at the fluffy clouds and notice that one particular cloud is slowly floating down towards you. You feel safe and loved as the cloud gently lands beside you and with a tiny bounce, settles. You realise that the cloud is there to take you to a special place.

◆ Climb onto the cloud and sink into the softness. The cloud feels warm and cosy as it gently carries you up into the air. Feel yourself floating upwards and upwards until the trees below are tiny; you feel so at peace as you realise you have been taken to a higher awareness and that all the answers you need are here.

◆ As you relax into your cloud, know that you can connect with your higher self. In your mind ask the questions you need answering to do with work. Ask the questions then lay back and allow the answers and creative potential to come to you.

◆ Ask what career would serve you best in the coming years. What career path will bring you the most fulfilment? Focus on your questions and receive the answers about what direction you should be heading in.

◆ When you have discovered all you need to know, let the cloud bring you gently back down onto the ground. As you alight from your cloud, feel a sense of direction and purpose as you focus on your future.

◆ Carry out the Closing Down technique, as outlined on page 44, to finish.

....

How I Used FLP to Plan My Own Book

In 2005, I took Paul McKenna five years into the future using FLP because he was curious about the process and wanted to experience it for himself. As I've said before, I can often catch glimpses of what other people are witnessing, and we both saw Paul in America working on a huge television show. For some reason he looked bigger, not fatter, just bigger. I told him, 'I can see your books and CDs flying off the shelves too, and there seems to be some conversation about the size of your dressing room for your TV show.'

Paul had the same images as me. He beamed as he said, 'Well, I shall just have to wait for the call from the States.'

Two weeks later it came when a top American TV producer called Paul and asked, 'When are you next in the States? I've heard about your work and I think you would go down a storm here.' Within one month it had started to happen. Paul began work on his top-rating TV show and everything began to fall into place. His contract stipulated that he should have a big dressing room and his manager, Claire, told me, 'Funny, but when he's in LA he's in the gym every day. I can see him getting bigger by the week.'

While Paul was looking five years into the future I cheekily asked him, 'What I am doing?' he replied, 'You have a book out. Wow, it's selling really well.'

A short time later while Paul was in LA discussing his show he called me up and said, 'Let's find out some more about that book of yours. Over the phone Paul guided me to five years into the future. He told me, 'You have a copy of your book in your hand – what is it called?'

'*Instant Intuition,* I replied without hesitation, and I promise you that is how I came up with the title for my first book. It came straight into my head. I downloaded it. Paul then asked me the subject of each chapter and what the cover looked like. I told him, 'Hey, I think I have had a face lift – I am looking a lot younger.' At the time I had no idea how images can be professionally retouched.

Two weeks later, I went to the wedding of celebrated healer Seka Nikolic. I chatted to a group of people including her literary agent, Robert Kirby, who asked me, 'So Anne, are you thinking of writing any books?'

'Funny you should ask that,' I replied. I told Robert about *Instant Intuition*. That night I got myself an agent.

Notice how quickly it all happened. It wasn't within five years that the book was published – it was 18 months. Somehow, once we know our path it opens up right before us, fast-tracking us towards our most attractive future options. Also notice how the creative information was almost given to me. I had been making notes for my book for some time but by viewing the outcome I removed the blocks and could then move ahead.

Thanks to FLP, I have a clear sense of my career direction. Also, by connecting with the future I somehow feel more centred. By having experienced 'what can be' I've a confident air about me that I've noticed my clients also possess.

There are so many ways to use Future Life Progression with business and creativity. You may have a keen interest in music and use FLP to move forward to see what the new trend will be for pop groups (e.g. previous trends have included boy bands, acoustic artists and heavy metal spoof groups). Imagine if years ago you had found Robbie Williams or the Spice Girls, or if you had spotted how successful rap music would become and had signed unknown singers who you knew would be hip-hop stars.

Maybe you are interested in art and need to know what markets to invest in and what will be worth a fortune in years to come. Or maybe you are a buyer – knowing what people will want in fashion, shoes and even furniture is a lucrative gift for your own career and the companies who employ you. Having your finger on the pulse could make you a millionaire.

All the exercises in this chapter can be adapted according to your needs. My advice is to practise them, so you get used to hooking into the process quickly, and check your success rate. Make a note of property hot spots when you ride the Magic Carpet, then scan the property pages to see if any of your FLP forecasting comes to fruition and when. With trend-spotting, and the Café exercise, again jot down key words and more detail if you have time to record what you see about future fashions for your chosen field.

Now you have learnt about trends, we will step up a level in Chapter 6 and face your repeating patterns – then learn how to break free of them. You are about to take control of your destiny.

CHAPTER 6
Dealing with Repeating Patterns

When I was 18 I went backpacking, travelling from Istanbul to Afghanistan before making my way to India on the now-famous Magic Bus. The bus visited unusual and exotic far flung places like India and Afghanistan, on what became known as the hippie trail, and was used by the more adventurous travellers in the seventies. While I was in the East I had my mind opened to the idea of reincarnation. Like many other people at that time, I started to look to Eastern beliefs for answers to the big questions, such as 'What happens when we die?' and 'Have we lived before?' These Eastern religions, Buddhism and Hinduism, began to provide me with the answers and they resonated deep with me. One of the main concepts that I came across at this time was reincarnation.

The idea of reincarnation opened up a whole new world for me. For the first time in my life I discovered that maybe there was more to life than I realised. It also made a lot of sense, especially when I thought about people who were born into suffering. As I learnt more about the subject my curiosity grew stronger, but it was much later that my interests took a new turn and I became aware of the possibility of future lifetimes. In a way, it should have been obvious. If we'd had past lives then why not future lives? But somehow the idea had not occurred to me then.

What is Reincarnation?

Reincarnation is the belief that there is a spark of energy or spirit – some call this the soul – that is the real 'us', and our earthly body is just a carriage for the soul's experiences in this lifetime. The soul moves on after we die to another life and each time it learns new lessons to help it progress spiritually. Reincarnation is one of the most ancient and widely held beliefs throughout the world. The word reincarnation comes from the Latin prefix 're', which means to repeat, and 'carnis', which means flesh. So literally, reincarnation means 'to be made flesh again.'

Until the 20th century, most people in the West believed that we had just one life and once we died we went to heaven, hell or purgatory. However, reincarnation was actually part of the Christian doctrine until 553 AD, when the council of Constantinople decreed it a heretical doctrine. During the 12th century, a Christian sect in France known as the Cathars formed and one of their main beliefs was that people lived over and over again, and in their many lifetimes the soul learnt important lessons. The Christian establishment was so against this idea that the group was annihilated by the inquisition during the 13th century.

Over the centuries, there have been many fierce debates about whether The Bible mentions rebirth. Many scriptures from both Old and New Testament are said to refer to the idea that after death we are reborn in another body. One of the strongest passages I feel is the following: 'Nicodemus said unto him [Christ], "How can anyone be born after having grown old? Can one enter a second time into the mother's womb and be born?" Jesus answered, "Very truly, I tell you."' Christ then goes on to express surprise that Nicodemus as a teacher of Israel did not understand this idea of being reborn again on earth (John 3:1–10).

There are also many references in The Bible to karma (the concept that what goes around comes around and that your actions will come back to you) such as 'Whatever one sows, that he will also reap' (Galatians 6:7) and '. . .then Jesus said to him (Peter), "Put your sword back in its place; for all who take the sword will perish by the sword."' (Matthew 26:52). And who can forget the classic, 'An eye for an eye and a tooth for a tooth' (Exodus 21:23–27) which certainly seems to say that we get back what we give out, and something I can strongly identify with, as I'm sure you can too.

Escaping Repeating Patterns

Have you ever seen the film *Groundhog Day*? Bill Murray plays Phil Connors, a TV weatherman who finds himself repeating the same day over and over again. At first he uses it as an excuse to behave badly, but after a while it helps him to review his life and what is important to him. He learns a great deal from the experience.

We don't have the opportunity to relive the same day over and over, but with Future Life Progression we can have the same overview by looking into our past, present and future lives, and seeing the real picture. By standing back and reviewing and previewing our soul journeys we can see where we have made, and will make, the same mistakes again or maybe see where opportunities have been missed. In fact, it's not unusual for events in my client's lives to baffle them until they go through this process. They tell me they have no idea why they experience bad luck or good luck and, as one American TV producer said, 'It feels like karma is one crazy lady.'

My clients also struggle to make sense of their emotions and why they feel a particular way. Often they feel stuck in a rut, or attract the same negative situation to themselves again and again – and this can happen in all areas of life. Some of the repeating patterns I've helped clients escape from are:

◆ Eating disorders

◆ Money issues – everything from getting into debt to investing in the wrong business

◆ A lack of decisiveness – always procrastinating and never making confident decisions

◆ Being plagued by headaches, or other unexplained health problems

◆ Addictions such as compulsive gambling and alcoholism

◆ Suffering from an inability to connect with others and feeling isolated and lonely

◆ Love – choosing the wrong type of partner again and again

After having their lives nearly ruined, I've helped clients turn their situation around and break away from their repeating patterns. In this chapter, I hope to help you identify your repeating patterns and give you the tools you need so you, too, can break free quickly and painlessly.

The Karmic Sandwich

So far in this book you've learnt how to look at your own future in a one-dimensional way using techniques like The Gallery and The Crystal Tower to go forward in time. Now that you have mastered these methods, I'm going to teach you how to use Future Life Progression to identify patterns that appear in your own past, present and future lives. I call this whole process The Karmic Sandwich. By studying your own Karmic Sandwich (your past, present and future) you will be able to identify patterns that plague you lifetime after lifetime. Unless you tackle these issues – this karma – it will continue to create a barrier to your spiritual development. But once you know about the patterns you can release them, or at least put them to one side until the time is right to deal with them.

In the coming pages I'm going to show you how to:

1   Identify your repeating patterns, using a method called The Word (see page 156)

2   Break free from your repeating patterns, using The Karmic Roundabout (see page 160)

3   Escape the bonds of abuse, using the Breaking Free exercise (see page 169)

4   Turn a negative into a positive – discover how you can move on from painful experiences, using a technique you already know, The Crystal Tower, and a version of The Doors.

Identify your Repeating Patterns

The first part of the process uses an exercise called The Word to help you identify your repeating patterns – and you can do this just by focusing on your question whilst in a relaxed state. Try not to edit your answers – your first instant thought contains the information you need.

....

The Word

◆ Carry out the Opening Up technique, as outlined on page 42, to begin.

◆ Think of at least one problem that has been a reoccurring issue in your current lifetime. Spend a few minutes reflecting on how and when this problem occurred, then write down the issue in a notebook or your journal (see page 28). Represent the issue with just one single word, for example 'money'.

◆ Next, I want you to breathe deeply in and out and relax. Ask yourself the question, 'What am I meant to learn from this situation?' and take the first thought that comes into your head. Write down the answer in your notebook.

◆ Try not to edit your thoughts, no matter how ridiculous they seem.

◆ Do the Closing Down exercise, as outlined on page 44, to end.

....

Common Repeating Patterns

Everyone has at least one issue and below I have listed briefly the areas that crop up the most during workshops and consultations – and the common karmic explanations or lessons to be learnt that accompany each problem. You may find your own issue (the repeating pattern pinpointed in The Word exercise you have just done, for example). However, this is by no means an exhaustive list. There isn't the space to go into great detail here, but this information will give you a pointer to start exploring on your own.

Eating Too Much or Too Little
Eating too much could stem from a past life in which you starved or were constantly hungry. Eating too little often comes from a past life in which you were put under great pressure to look a certain way, or were only valued for you looks. Now in our current society where being slim is highly regarded you may be putting yourself under too much pressure to be 'the thinnest'.

Money Worries
Maybe your pattern is that you get back on your feet financially only to find that a year later you are in the same boat, and up to your ears in debt with very little **money**. This is usually a sign that you have had many lifetimes of poverty and recreate them in your current life.

Suffering Abuse
Perhaps you have a reccurring issue with people mistreating you (professionally and privately). Maybe those around you

don't take you seriously, or respect you, or the **abuse** manifests as people simply taking you for granted. Usually you will have been in a lowly position in the past, maybe a slave or servant. The other option is you may have been wealthy and misused your wealth and have agreed to come back this time to learn how to use your money wisely. Or maybe you were a powerful person that misused your authority. This past life can sometimes result in authority figures in your current life being hard on you, or finding that career advancement slips through your fingers, stopping you from once again being in authority. Whatever the situation, it needs to be released.

Restlessness

Many of my clients who have found it hard to hold down a job have simply been carrying old past-life patterns. If you experience **restlessness**, or an unexplained need to keep moving on, it could be because in a past life you were a nomad, a gypsy or maybe a pioneer searching for new lands. One of my clients was a wandering minstrel; no wonder the average factory job drove him crazy with boredom.

Attracting the Wrong Partner

Julie, a client of mine, kept attracting men who were gamblers. Time and again she would find herself bailing them out financially and getting them into therapy – simply for them to get on their feet then leave her. Julie tried mixing in different circles because she wondered if it was the type of place she socialised in that attracted this type. Finally, after meeting a man through church who turned out to be a compulsive online gambler, she realised that this was a pattern deep within her. She was attracting the **wrong partner**.

You may have a pattern like John, who had plenty of dates but none of the girls wanted to commit to him. All he wanted was a family yet every time he thought he had found the perfect girl she would tell him she 'needed space' or 'more time'.

You may find that you have a pattern of meeting partners who are unfaithful, bringing you trauma after trauma and resulting in low self-esteem and a mistrust of future relationships. This could be because you betrayed your partner in a past life – either romantically or financially – or perhaps because they have been unfaithful to you for many lifetimes before, and you have not ever dealt with it. Karma replays throughout our lifetimes until we learn the lesson. The pattern will occur again and again until you take control and stop the behavior by breaking free and move on.

How to Break Free

After identifying one of your particular problems from the list above, or whole myriad issues, it's time to move onto The Karmic Roundabout. The Karmic Roundabout can be used for any issue at all. In fact, you can use this simple visualisation as the first step in breaking the patterns that blight your life. The negative pattern may be a situation, or having a certain type of person in your life, or perhaps your own behaviour or lack of self-belief.

Although it's simple, the exercise is very powerful because it works on a deep level and contains intention. As anyone working with energy knows, intention is the first step to creation. Here you are going to walk away from your past and create the foundations for a sparkling new future.

....

The Karmic Roundabout

You can do this exercise for one issue at a time. This will really help you to focus on the pattern and sever your links with its energy.

◆ Carry out the Opening Up technique, as outlined on page 42, to begin.

◆ Think of the reoccurring problems that you have had in your current lifetime (money problems, romances that have gone wrong or maybe people not respecting you, for example).

◆ Pick one issue and link in with the energy of this pattern by re-playing one of its scenarios in your mind. For example, your bullying boss shouting at you.

◆ Now imagine that you are stepping onto a merry-go-round that turns very slowly. Each time you come to a certain point as you go round the problem reoccurs, again and again. Know that this is what happens not just in your current life but has done so in the past, and will keep occurring in your future life unless you take action.

◆ I want you to know that all you have to do is step off the roundabout and the pattern will be broken. See the round-about moving round. Take a deep breath and step off, leaving the negative energy behind.

◆ By stepping off the roundabout, the wheel of karma, you have acknowledged the pattern and have released it. Now it's up to you to continue to act on this positive energy and remain free.

◆ Carry out the closing down technique, as outlined on page 44, to finish.

....

Some of you may need to do The Karmic Roundabout exercise more than once. Most people do clear their issue in one visualisation, but occasionally little reminders trigger old patterns. For example, you could have had a problem with a family member – say for instance, your father – and you use the karmic roundabout to clear the issue. But when you visit him old memories begin to stir and a trace of the old patterning appears. As soon as you have the space and peace to do the visualisation, simply jump back on the roundabout and clear the fragments. Each time you do this it will get easier and easier until one day you simply cannot feel the pattern at all.

Overcoming restlessness

As well as teaching the techniques in this book to my clients, I also use them regularly myself. As you may have gathered, I have a busy mind and a restless nature and, in some respects, it has served me well. It has always pushed me to look for new things, to learn, to explore and travel. But there was a time when I just couldn't sit still. My spiritual mentor, Greta, used to say, 'Anne, just be.' This was one of my hardest lessons. I would ask her, 'What do you mean, just *be*? I have things to do. I might miss out on something, I can't just sit around.' She would laugh and tell me to be comfortable in my own space and allow things to come to me rather than me chase things. It took me a long time to learn that lesson.

Now if I feel restless I use the Karmic Roundabout and leave the restlessness behind. As I step off the roundabout I feel at peace, because using this technique gives me a calmness. Greta was right – whatever was making me restless would work itself out, or if I needed something it would come to me. Often the phone would ring within minutes of doing this exercise with an answer or someone offering just what I needed.

Roberta is a good example of someone with a deep rooted karmic pattern which was affecting her life. She was anorexic. When she walked into my office she looked so fragile and as she opened up to me, she revealed this was the first time she had ever talked to anyone about her eating disorder. (Roberta had been recommended to me by her friend, Jane, who I had treated for bulimia. I am trained in clinical hypnotherapy and coaching techniques – and so I treated Jane's problem in a few sessions.)

But Roberta was different. My instincts told me that the anorexia stretched back a lot further than just this particular soul journey. I asked the young woman about her life now and she told me how she had enjoyed a good upbringing, although her mother was quite neurotic about food. A neurotic parent is enough to give anyone an eating disorder, but still I had the niggling feeling that the cause ran deeper.

I took Roberta into an altered state and instructed her to go back to the very first time she had experienced a problem with food. Her body tensed up as she began talking about being in a cave and the whole tribe fighting over the latest catch – her mother regularly took food from her. She was not strong and often went hungry.

This lifetime confirmed to me that this pattern had been around many, many times. Rather than dig into every single painful karmic memory, I took the young woman forward to see how she would be in her next lifetime. Roberta immediately began talking about being in a remote place with little food – yet again. It was time to clear this pattern and I decided to use The Karmic Roundabout (see page 160).

I told Roberta to focus on the problems she had with eating and to know that we were about to resolve the issue. Together we imagined standing on the roundabout and coming to a certain point. Whenever another memory occurred, her mother was there somewhere, reinforcing the pattern.

From the moment her mother had snatched the food away from her in the cave a pattern had developed that had reoccurred many times. Roberta saw herself as a poor French peasant woman working for a rich bullying woman, and yes, you've guessed it – her mother again. Repeatedly we saw snapshots or snippets of information, and these were all we needed to hook into the life pattern and clear it by getting off the roundabout. There was no benefit for Roberta to relive the hardship she had suffered – we simply wanted to clear it once and for all. As Roberta stepped off the roundabout she gave a big sigh and a huge grin beamed across her face. She said, 'I'm hungry – I think I will go and have a good lunch when I get home.'

We had cleared the problem, but just to make sure, I took Roberta for a little journey into the future using The Gallery (see page 52). We peeped at her in five years' time and there she was' sitting around a table with her still-to-come children enjoying a hearty meal. She was happy, healthy and there was no sign of the problem that had worn her down for so many lifetimes. She won't be passing on her eating disorder to her children, either, which is another major positive outcome from her session.

Case study

Felicity told me, 'I'm a smart and educated woman, but I just can't understand why every few years I find myself in serious debt. I've worked in highly paid jobs, which I've lost through one reason or another, and I've even married a rich man who left me and hid his money. Then I started a business that now looks as if it will fail. I'm desperate for an answer.'

All became clear when Felicity saw a series of past lives using The Gallery. Instead of looking at her lives in the future, she saw pictures of past lives on the wall and jumped into them to pick up the details. It seems that every time she had a wealthy life things went wrong, but when she was poor she was happier. She told me, 'Wow, it looks as if I am allergic to having money.'

I did some therapy work with her using coaching techniques to integrate the happiness and the wealth, enabling her to now experience both. Felicity's business turned around and is now making plenty of money. We even went five years into the future with FLP to check up on her success and stability – and all was well. She told me, 'A few years ago I would never have thought of using FLP to help me. But there's no doubt in my mind that whatever block I had has gone and I feel like a money magnet, it's brilliant.'

Escaping the Bonds of Abuse

Debt can be debilitating, but an even worse pattern to repeat is that of abuse. Imagine finding out that someone has ill-treated you not only in your current lifetime but over and again, stretching back years into the past. Imagine still that you don't clear this energy and even in your future lifetimes you still have the same problem. Clearing these patterns will change your life and clear the way for respect and love to come your way.

Abuse can be one of the most hardest cycles to escape as one client Barbara, in her mid 50s, discovered again in this particular life, this soul journey.

She and John had been childhood sweethearts and married at 19. Barbara came from a family with loving parents and John's father, Pat, was a good hard-working man – until he drank. As soon as there was any pressure, Pat disappeared to the pub, returning home late, drunk and abusive.

Unfortunately, once they were married and saving up for a house John began to drink just like his father. At first it was a few pints after work, but soon John would be there at closing time. Three months after marrying they had their first serious row. Barbara was upset; she had been working overtime and saving and felt she was watching their money being poured into a pint glass.

Most couples row at some point. Some do it regularly and feel that it clears the air. The difference was on this occasion John hit Barbara full across her face, leaving her with a fat bleeding lip. She was horrified.

The following day John wept as he pleaded forgiveness. For the first time he talked about how as a little boy he had to watch his father hitting his mother and he was powerless to save her.

'He told me he would do anything to make amends,' said Barbara. So she and John had some long talks, and because she knew about his upbringing she felt deep in her heart that John just needed some love.

After this first incident things settled down. John worked hard and they saved their money. Then John's mother suddenly died. He was beside himself with grief. All his guilt from not being able to help her through her troubled times came to the surface and John began drinking heavily again. On the night before his mother's funeral he hit the bottle and Barbara – leaving a large bruise on her cheekbone.

She told me, 'I will never forget the looks of the other people at the funeral. Everyone could see he had hit me. John had been oblivious, he was so drunk. He didn't remember a thing.'

Sadly, this was a long line of drunken beatings that Barbara endured. Twenty years later nothing much had changed accept they had a daughter who Barbara tried to shield from the beatings. John had convinced her over and over again that things would get better; he even had counselling for two years. But if anything the counselling seemed to be giving him permission to wallow. John drank less often but when he did the abuse and violence was worse. He would slur, 'My counsellor says it's your fault I drink, you don't do enough for me. If you were more of a wife to me I'd be happier.'

Barbara knew the counsellor had said no such thing. Twenty years of John had taught her just how much he could twist anything when he was in one of his moods. 'I've come for this Future Life Progression because I need to know if things will be better in the future with John. I can see fear in our daughter's eyes. I can see shame when she has to face people who have seen him drunk in the street. For her sake this has to stop. He drinks less often since he began the counselling I need to know that one day we will have a nice life together.'

My instincts told me to take Barbara to the ten-year point. Often I can see what my clients can see. I knew she needed to know the truth. As she jumped into the picture in her own Gallery she gasped and said, 'Oh no, he is just as bad – no, he's worse. He no longer has counselling and he drinks every night.'

'What's happening in your daughter's life?' I said.

'She is engaged to a nice young chap. He's hard-working.'

'Is he good to her?' Barbara's face suddenly froze, 'Oh God, he drinks. He is being nasty to her.'

'Barbara, what is the message from your future self to your current self?' I asked.

She replied, 'If I stay with John, Kirsty will follow my pattern.'

'Let's look at how things will be in your future lifetime.'

'I'm with John again. We look very happy. He is working at a nuclear plant. I'm a nurse. The hospital looks very high tech, things are going well, oh until–' Barbara gave a shudder, 'they're closing down the nuclear plant. John, or Bill as he is in this life, will be out of work. Oh no, he is drinking. Does this never end?'

At that point Barbara's eyes began flickering wildly. 'What can you see, Barbara?'

She replied, 'This is shocking. I don't know where all this is coming from. I'm going back in time. I can see John's granddad hitting his grandma. I can see generation after generation in the past with the same pattern. It's as if I can see history laid out like a long carpet going back to as far as we can see with the drinking and violence.

'But the scary things is I can see it happening to my own grandchildren. This has to stop, and it has to stop right now.'

Everything Barbara saw was also before my own eyes. I also

had images of her and her husband in a past life. They had been natives living in the Amazon jungle. John would drink a type of fermented sap from a tree and go into a trance-like state; wild-eyed, he would shriek that he'd been taken over by a demon. You can guess the rest, Barbara would suffer violence again.

FLP can help us to make decisions, but it can also help us to break free of patterns. Who wants to get to the end of their life and look back with lots of regrets? Within a month of the progression Barbara had left John and moved out, taking her daughter with her. John had always controlled the money so she left with very little and went to a refuge. A few months later the council gave them a small flat and a grant to buy some furniture. She told me, 'John has pleaded and begged and told me he would go back to counselling, but it's no use. Once you know you have had this lifetime after lifetime and even seen yourself hundreds of years into the future still suffering, it's a shocking wake-up call. But the biggest factor in all of this was seeing my daughter go through the same. There's no way I'm going to let this happen.'

Two years later Barbara met and married a kind and gentle man. Barbara called me to tell me the news and said, 'If I'd not had the Future Life Progression I doubt I'd ever have left John. Thank you so much for your help.'

Abusive relationships can run through families who repeat the same patterns over and over again – attracting the same type of partner with the same issues. Not only do we need to clear the karmic ties, we also need to clear our own ancestral patterns. The breaking free exercise below will deal with these patterns, no matter where they have originated. Gaining a blast of pure universal energy, you will feel energised and ready to move forward into a more positive and happy future.

Breaking Free

◆ Carry out the Opening Up exercise, as outlined on page 42, to begin.

◆ Find yourself a comfy place and allow your breathing to deepen. Focus on the issue you wish to break free from. Think of a word to represent this problem. For instance, if the issue is to do with money, think of the word 'money'.

◆ Imagine writing the word on a piece of paper. Let go of the piece of paper and watch it float up into the sky and beyond. Know that it will reach the universe where it will be dealt with, and that you will gain all the help you need.

◆ Now ask the universe for help: 'Universe, please take my problem and let it be healed. Bring me peace and remove anything in its way.' You might not feel it, but the universe will give you a blast of pure universal energy. You have asked for help and you will receive help.

◆ Repeat this request three times then add, 'Thank you Universe for your help, protection and love.'

◆ Having sent a message to the Universe, I now want you to become aware of your body and allow it to feel light and floaty. Your arms and legs feel lighter and lighter and your head and torso feel as if they are floating. Feel yourself becoming weightless and imagine that you are actually floating upwards, higher and higher, until you are looking down at the houses and roads. You can see trees and a stream and still you float higher and higher.

- The houses become smaller and smaller until they disappear and the roads become fainter and fainter and still you rise. Up and up you go until you can make out countries, then continents, then the whole world.

- Look down on the world and wonder at its beauty. What can you see? Oceans and countries, mountains and rivers. Whole continents appear before you. They support millions of people each and every day, renewing and replenishing themselves and the people who live there.

- As you look down on the world, imagine that you had never been born. How different would the world be? Would it carry on as usual? Would it notice you were never there?

- Now think about the people who have been in your life. How different would their lives have been if there had never been a you?

- As you look down and watch the world go about its business, feel at peace as you know that everything will carry on just the same whether you are there or not. What will be, will be. You have no worries.

- As you look down on your world, what advice would you give yourself? Take a few moments to connect to your higher self and listen to his or her message, which is given with love.

- Be aware that you are here in this life for just a short space of time. To the world you are just a brief visitor – someone who stops by for a while as the world continues spinning and evolving in its own right. Be aware of what is truly important to the world and to you in this lifetime.

◆ Remember that you are free. You are free from past karmic bonds in this life and the ones before, and you will be free in the future.

◆ Carry out the Closing Down exercise, as outlined on page 44, to finish.

....

You can use this exercise for any type of powerful pattern linked to the emotions, be it abuse and even addictions (food, shopping, drugs, for example). Had I met John, Barbara's ex-husband (see her case study on page 165), I would have suggested doing this exercise and inserting the word 'drink', firstly on his imaginary piece of paper and, secondly, in the affirmation asking the Universe for help. I would then have suggested that he also repeat the exercise to sever his karmic ties connected to violence, this time using the word 'violence' on his imagined piece of paper and again in the affirmation to the Universe.

Case study

Joe visibly shook as he told me his story. He was a compulsive gambler and so far it had cost him his business and his first marriage. He confessed, 'The way things are going, I am about to lose my second wife and my home. Yet I just can't stop. I have heard about your work and to be honest I don't see how you can help me. This is my last resort.'

With such skepticism I wondered if he would be a good subject, but Joe was so determined to find the cause of his problems he followed my instructions. He relaxed then floated back to a previous life in Greece using The Gallery (see page 52). 'I am gambling, only this time I am the bookie. I have loaded dice and I am cheating people. They cannot complain because they shouldn't be doing this. It is frowned upon.'

'How do you feel about what you are doing?'

'I love it. My dice are loaded and I smile every time I find another idiot. These people will believe anything. They keep coming back for more.'

'Do you never feel bad about what you are doing?' I asked.

'Never. I also make predictions for them and do something that is like 'find the lady', a three card trick used to con people out of money, where I use sleight of hand. It is too easy.' he smirked.

Wondering if he ever got his comeuppance in that lifetime, I asked Joe if things eventually went wrong for him. 'No not at all,' he smiled. 'In fact, rich and powerful people court me to ask my advice. It is hilarious.'

This surprised me. Usually, I find that at some point something happens to make them realise the error of their ways. No wonder Joe was driven to gamble; it had served him well in his past life. In his present life, there was a part of him trying to find the easy life through this method once again. I brought Joe back and asked more about his current life. As he talked, it became clear that the karmic repercussion had finally caught up with him. His first wife left him and took everything they owned; his last business partner cheated him. He sighed, 'I feel as if I am the unluckiest person in the world.' I explained to Joe about how he had reaped bad karma, but he simply didn't understand. He told me, 'I still feel as if I just need one good win to get me on a winning streak and back on track.'

Let's look at your future,' I told him. I took Joe forward to his next lifetime and true to form, there he was, gambling – only this time with the stock market and the family fortune. Again the cocksure edge was there. 'My family are worried, but I know what I am doing. Wait and see – I will make their fortune even bigger. Besides, they have plenty.' I kept moving Joe forward and the big bucks never arrive. Each time he sounded a little less confident until finally he saw himself as an old man living in poverty.

I then asked Joe to float out of his body and look down at the sad sight of him as an elderly man in his future lifetime. I asked him, 'So what can you learn from this?'

There was a trace of a sob in his voice as he said, 'Really, I need so little in life. Why do I do this? There are so many things that are so much more important in life.'

'So where do you go from here?'

'I need to make amends. '

'What will happen if you stay on your current path?'

Joe gave a shudder as he said, 'For a second there I felt as if the old man in the future actually touched me and sent me a feeling. Does that sound crazy? I actually physically felt something inside me that showed me the futility of my actions.'

I guided him through the Breaking Free exercise (see page 169) and it had a powerful effect as for the first time aloud he acknowledged that he wanted to break free from his gambling addiction. Joe was quiet as he left my office – I could see he had a lot to think about. He called me some months later to say he hadn't thought about gambling once. He told me, 'This is weird, but I feel as if the Joe who gambled was someone else. It's

almost as if this is the real me, not him.' He was now planning
to train as a therapist to help others to stop gambling.

Karma and Punishment

I don't believe we are here to be punished, no matter what we
have done in the past, and I truly believe we can all wipe the
slate clean at any time simply by leading a good life this time
round. The techniques in this chapter can speed up the process
and your spiritual development and also save you a lot of pain
in this life – and your next.

*Knowledge is power. The more you discover about your past
and future the more you can make choices that will best serve
your current time.*

Turning a Negative into a Positive

The first time I met Cindy she bounced into my office, and within
10 minutes had told me how she had self-harmed and been
abused by her stepfather. She was someone who most definitely
had suffered a lot of negative experiences. Often when people
disclose such personal information so early upon meeting, they
are almost wearing their misfortunes as an identity badge. But
Cindy was different; she wanted to feel better and to help other
youngsters going through what she had suffered as a child.

As a young Asian woman she felt such problems were very hidden in her culture. She told me, 'In my area, Asian youngsters have nowhere to go if they are being abused. I would love to help them in some way, but I don't know how I can do this.' Cindy also told me she was single and added, 'I have issues with trust, and I have never had a real sexual relationship because of what happened to me when I was little.'

It's hard hearing such information but I was determined to bring light into her world. I hoped that FLP would help her to move forward so she could help herself to help others. Using The Crystal Tower (see page 54) I took her forward five years and she saw herself living in the countryside with a baby daughter. Her husband was by her side – he seemed shy and very supportive. As she spoke, Cindy had an air of purpose and confidence about her. Her future self seemed finally at peace.

She told me, 'I have become an author and written several books to help others who had suffered from child abuse. I am planning to take my work in this field a lot further too, so I need to look ahead.'

At her request, I took her to the ten-year point. Cindy had achieved her aims. She was now well known internationally and had made a difference to the lives of many youngsters. Cindy had developed guidelines of best practice for dealing with sexual abuse victims and was in talks with the UN to highlight the situation in certain countries. She had set up grass root support groups, which had become firmly established as beacons of help for those in need. The woman had fought to get her message across and now, because she had helped so many people, she led the way and as a result had become quite an icon. I had images in my head that told me she had relocated, too, to a different country. I asked her, 'Where are you living?'

She replied, 'It's not England. I am in a wonderful house.'

I asked her if the house was high up and overlooking a city. Astonished, she told me that it was. We could both see the same image. We could both also see that she now had a little boy. It was like watching a movie with a friend as we chatted about what was in front of us. We both saw, and confirmed, that she had done considerable work with youngsters all over the world.

Cindy said, 'There are some people who are critical of my work. This doesn't surprise me, especially as some of them are the male elders in the Asian community who would prefer this type of thing to be left underground and hidden.'

As we moved forward into her future life she told me, 'I am a young woman, but I do not understand – I am seeing several images at once. I feel I am talking to lots of people, sort of guiding them but at the same time I am standing out in nature. I am inside and outside both at the same time.'

I told her, 'This is something I have seen before. You are not human, you are a light being. You are seeing yourself talking to thousands of people?'

She replied, 'Yes I am, but I do not see how that is possible.'

I immediately had the answer. I told her, 'This is a holographic image of yourself. As you have developed so much in your current lifetime and have found your spiritual path, you will be highly evolved in your next lifetime and you will continue to help others.'

A negative ended up with a positive result for Cindy, not just in this life but in the next. I've come across other clients, too, who have turned something that would crush others into a positive outcome, for example someone who was bullied at work and left to run their own business. They now earn three times their previous salary. The following short exercise will help you to turn something dark into something light.

Turning Darkness into Light

If you have areas of your life that have given you lots of problems or upset, you can change negative events into positive events simply by using this version of The Doors exercise (see page 85) to find alternative futures and better choices. Remember to do the Opening Up and Closing Down exercises to begin and end (see pages 42, 44).

◆ As you walk through each door, take time to decide which is your best option. Stop and feel where you are happiest. Which door is best for your long-term future? Which door takes you to a place of most contentment? Which door gives you the most control over your destiny? One option will stand out from the others and show you a better life.

Once you have done this, as a 'thank you' to the Universe, find a way to help others who have had the same problem. Even if you just donate a little time or money to a charity, this will help to bring more positive energy to the world and the victims.

As you discover more about yourself, your current life, your past and your future lives, you will become more in tune with the essence that is your soul. This is the part of you that is eternal, full of wisdom and which understands and knows all.

Now that you have cleared patterns from your past and connected with your future, you are ready for the next level. In the following chapter you will discover the reason you are here and the reason you exist. You are going to connect with your soul's purpose, your spiritual blueprint for this life.

CHAPTER 7
Finding Your Soul's Purpose

Most people are unaware of their soul's purpose, yet this is the one part of their being, or spirit, that is constant. Whether you believe or not in life after death, your soul certainly does! In this chapter I'm going to help you to find your soul's purpose, which in turn will not only give you a feeling of contentment and calmness, but will help you progress spiritually.

Discover:

◆ Your soul's purpose and what it means

◆ Soul lessons – why we go through different experiences and need to learn lessons

◆ Life reviews – what happens when we 'die'

◆ Why it's important to find your soul's purpose

◆ How you can tell if you have already found your soul's purpose – your spiritual checklist

◆ Lost your soul's purpose? How to get back on track spiritually

◆ Using Future Life Progression to discover, to link in, with your soul's purpose

What is Your Soul's Purpose?

Your soul has one true purpose: to evolve and grow to become one with the universal energy – the energy that runs through everything, is part of everything and governs all things. We can only achieve this growth by learning what we need to learn, and the best way to do this is to take human form and work our way through the hustle and bustle that is life.

Everyone's soul has a purpose and everyone has a role to play in the game of life – we are all connected. One person's purpose may be to save the rain forest, whereas another individual's may be to look after one particular person as an unpaid carer. No one's purpose is more important than anyone else's soul's purpose. I have an aunt who swears her purpose in life is to clean. She is never without a damp cloth in her hand, so perhaps she is right!

Your purpose, your role, is the reason you exist in this lifetime. Each lifetime will teach you and allow you opportunities to perfect yourself until the time when you are ready to reconnect with the universal energy. This is when you have learnt all you need to learn.

Often I meet people who tell me that they have the most wonderful life, with a loving partner, success, health and beautiful children, yet they feel there is a missing piece of the jigsaw. I always know that it is their soul's purpose they need to find, and that once they have this they will feel complete.

Soul Lessons

Often the people around us provide our soul lessons, and indeed when we are between lives we decide what we need to learn and who will best teach us our lessons. We in turn teach others what they need to know – spiritual agreements are made, which is why certain people come into your life. So the next time you feel exasperated by your bitchy sister or selfish brother, know that you asked for them to appear in this soul journey in order for you to learn from them.

Maybe from your bitchy sister you learn that you are meant to give her love to soften her – or you need to learn to turn the other cheek or even to tell her where to go. Perhaps with your selfish brother your soul lesson is to give him what he needs so that he can realise it is not what he wants after all. Maybe you are to teach him how to give by example, or perhaps you need to learn to be patient – it is for you to work out which lesson you need to practice and master.

Life Reviews: What Happens When we 'Die'

Before we enter each soul journey (ie being born on earth) we undergo a life review, assessing what we have and haven't learnt in our previous life. We do this review with the elders, spiritual beings who care for us and guide us. There is no blame – simply the chance to review our progress and then discuss what we need to learn and how best to learn it in our next lifetime. Our soul's purpose is born in this discussion with our guides on the spiritual plane. Throughout our life, we will be given clues to our soul's purpose in the form of déjà vu, synchronicity, or coincidence, to nudge us in the right direction and jog our memories.

Why it is Important to Find Your Soul's Purpose

Think about what would happen if you did not find your soul's purpose. You would move from one life to another repeating the same patterns, endlessly round and round with the same problems, upsets and anguish. Perhaps your soul purpose would be to bring peace – and once you knew this, you could work at bringing peace. You may do this on a small scale and mediate in family conflicts, teaching your siblings and parents how to get along. You may study politics and promote peace on a grander scale. But if you do not know your purpose, you may go from life to life with conflict arriving at your door, getting involved in aggression rather than learning to work with this energy to turn negatives into positives. This is one reason why some people are aggressive or have a chip on their shoulder – they have become defensive after many lifetimes of conflict. Once they know their purpose, however, they can work to resolve it.

How to Tell if you Have Found Your Soul's Purpose

Read the list below to see if you can recognise any of these scenarios:

◆ You may have noticed patterns, as if being pushed by fate in a certain direction again and again. You may already realise what you need to do in order to grow.

◆ You will also be a natural at 'your soul's purpose' and doors of opportunity will have opened as if by magic. When you are on the right path, the right people appear in your life and whatever you need materialises, including opportunities, mentors and money.

◆ If you have found your soul's purpose you will have a feeling of completeness.

◆ If you are spiritually aware you may have already become aware of your purpose through dreams or meditations. Shortly, you will be doing a meditation that will guide you to your own soul purpose.

By just answering 'yes' to one of the bullet points you have already shown that you have recognised, or are in a position to recognise, your soul's purpose. However, you may need more guidance and the exercises in this chapter will help you to work towards achieving your soul's purpose.

If you don't recognise yourself in any of the scenarios, don't panic. I am about to help you find your spiritual path using a variety of easy techniques that will give you excellent guidance and get you back on track spiritually.

We are all here for a purpose and the following exercises will give you steps along the way towards fulfilling that purpose. You may discover the whole story or you may find part of it, but as you begin to follow your path, things will click into place and you will have a greater sense of wholeness. As we connect with our soul's purpose we gain a feeling of completeness.

Can your Soul Lose its Purpose?

It is possible to lose your way spiritually. You can become disconnected from your spiritual self by not having awareness of your soul's purpose, and you can lose a sense of your soul's purpose. But by following the guidelines in this chapter, and using the techniques, you will discover what you are meant to be experiencing.

If you have gone off track, you will find life keeps sending you problems – and these problems are sent to teach you something. This happened with one of my clients, Janice.

Throughout her whole life Janice wanted to be successful, but no matter how hard she worked she could only get so far before things went wrong. She told me, 'I started a driving business then broke my foot and couldn't drive. I opened a bar, then someone opened a bigger and better premises up the road and took all the custom. I could go on and on.'

Janice did the Soul to Soul exercise (see page 184) and discovered that part of her life path was to raise money for children in orphanages. She herself had lost both parents at an early age, which gave Janice her clue to her soul's purpose. Janice was lucky enough to be brought up by her loving aunt, but many children are not so fortunate.

Later, Janice opened another business, a bistro, and set up a monthly fund-raising evening for an orphanage overseas. She vowed to do this every month for the rest of her life. Her bistro business has thrived.

Now you can find your soul's purpose using a method I call Soul to Soul.

....

Soul to Soul

◆ Begin with the Opening Up technique, as outlined on page 42.

◆ Imagine you are out in nature on a beautiful summer evening. You feel at peace as you look around and see the world winding down, the birds beginning to quieten and the sun slowly fading. You stroll in a leisurely manner when you notice up ahead a small round vehicle.

◆ As you walk up to the vehicle you are surprised to see written on the door your name with the words 'Your Purpose'. You open the door and peek inside. The interior of the vehicle is cosy and glowing with a golden light. You step inside and feel safe and protected. You know this vehicle is very special and has come to help you on your soul journey. It has a familiar feeling and deep down, you know you have been inside this vehicle before at some point in your soul's journey.

◆ You sit down on a pile of comfy cushions. You know that this vehicle will take you to a higher level of awareness.

◆ Feel yourself rising up and up into the air with happiness and excitement. Somehow you know that this will be of great benefit to you. Somehow you know you are being taken to a great source of knowledge that will aid your soul's progress.

◆ The vehicle comes to a halt. The door slides open. Now step outside onto a platform and into a huge cavern. Look around. You feel quite tiny as you look up and down, yet still you feel safe. Again, you feel you have been here before.

◆ Behind you are three elders sitting on tall chairs. They smile and beckon you over. You know that they are your guides, your elders. They know and understand all. The elder in the centre tells you that they are about to show you snippets of your lifetimes past and future. She explains there are themes that you have experienced time after time, lessons that have needed to be learned. There are things that you can free yourself from once you know of them.

◆ She then explains that you have held yourself back from being all you can be. You have done this because of events that have happened in your lifetimes, but now you can be aware and release what doesn't serve you.

◆ With a wave of her hand, images begin to flicker onto the cavern wall. They are images of you in various lifetimes. The images may appear to you as an image on the cavern wall, or in your mind's eye; the information may come to you as thought forms or feelings. Allow the information to flow.

◆ Stay as long as you wish and notice what messages are here. What do you need to know? What do you need to release? What is your higher purpose? What has occurred for you time after time?

◆ When you have finished, the elder to the right points to an abyss and tells you that anything you no longer want or need can be thrown into the abyss. With a twinkle in his eye, he reassures you that you can put people into the abyss if they have held you back, but no harm will come to them. It is simply removing them from your soul path. You have work to do. You are now ready to be all you can be. You are ready to fulfill your soul purpose to release and move forward.

◆ The elder to your left sends you a beam of silvery energy to
   cleanse and energise you, and all three wave as you climb
   back abroad your vehicle and silently float away.

   As you arrive back in your current world you feel complete,
   whole. You feel like you – the real you.

◆ Finish with the Closing Down exercise (see page 44).

....

Using Future Life Progression to Link in with your Soul's Purpose

Sometimes you get those clients who have been there, done it
all and got the T-shirt. Sadie was one of those people, and it was
obvious that I was her last resort for a bit of clarity.

'There are so many things I've looked at, everything from
astrology to reflexology to palm reading,' Sadie confided, 'and
I'm still no clearer to which is right for me. I've no idea what I
should be doing with my life or what is my soul's purpose.'

I took Sadie back to a past life in which she described an incarnation on a Pacific island. She was a young girl with long dark
hair and wearing a sarong. She looked very peaceful as she sat
washing stones in a bubbling brook, then warming them in a
tiny pool at the base of a volcano. She then took them into a
nearby straw hut where she laid them as healing stones on the
back of a patient.

She told me, 'I have a feeling of total serenity. It is a feeling I
have never known before in my current life.'

This past life showed us that natural therapies were indeed
very much part of her soul work. As she said, 'This feels more
real than my current life. This feels more me.'

Sadie's future lifetime would help us confirm what we already thought – that she should train to be a holistic therapist.

Using The Gallery technique (see page 52) she jumped 100 years into the future, telling me, 'I look very similar to how I looked in my last lifetime, with long dark hair, but this time I am wearing a white coat. It is quite like a doctor's coat. I seem to be working some sort of a machine.' She laughed as she told me, 'It looks like a high-tech hairdryer. Hold on, it has a laser – I am aiming it at a patient.'

Sadie went on to tell me how the laser, this light beam, ran through a large crystal. She had never heard of this before, but this is something that comes up again and again in Future Life Progression sessions – many times my clients mention using lasers and crystals together to cure patients. They have all talked about incredible recoveries using this method.

Sadie's clients in this future life were also showing dramatic results. As she left my office she told me that she had no doubt at all that the course she was meant to take was one working with crystals. By discovering this one piece of vital information using Future Life Progression, Sadie could now begin to fulfil her soul's purpose.

Work you have done in past lives will come naturally to you in your current life, as in Sadie's case. This skill is also a part of us and is what people call 'a gift' or 'a knack'. If you have a hunch about your soul's purpose you can check your past lives, your future life say five years from now, and your future lifetime using The Gallery (see page 52).

Gem Therapy

Cutting-edge gem therapy, which combines the ancient knowledge of precious stones with space-age science, already exists. Electronic lamps, called the Lux IV, have been invented and fine-tuned by Dr Jon Whale over the past 20 years. The scientist combines the healing properties of gems with light, and these lamps can be used to treat a wide range of illnesses from depression to eczema. Go to www.whalemedical.com for more information.

Very often people feel that they may be on their path, but not quite. This is when frustrations set in – you may feel you are doing everything right, you are working hard and being good to others, so why is everything so difficult? This is when you need to use the Soul to Soul exercise (see page 184) to fine-tune the information. You can look into the future but sometimes you need the extra zing, that little spark that feels everything is just how it should be, to give you that final elusive piece of information to complete the picture and set your soul purpose into action.

Soul to Soul will fine-tune your path, giving you the exact information you need so that you can move forward with the confidence that you are doing exactly what you are meant to be doing. Doubts will leave you, and you will have a new sense of total confidence.

Case study

Recently a world famous pop star came to see me. On the surface he has everything he could possibly want – he has millions of pounds, he fills stadiums and girls love him – yet he wears a constant pained look on his face. He told me, 'A friend told me about the soul purpose work you do and we had a DIY session ourselves. I thought I would find the answer.'

He told me how he tried to send out positive messages to his young fans and that he had cleaned up his drug and drink problem. The famous celeb added, 'I realised I had a responsibility because youngsters copy me. I knew I needed to set a good example. I have changed my life so much I just cannot see what else I need to do.'

Something was still bothering him, though, and so we did a soul purpose session. He gained a clear vision that shocked him. He said it looked like a movie with a split screen. On one side he could see himself spending hundreds of dollars on bottles of expensive wine and wasting literally hundreds of thousands of pounds every week. The other side of the screen showed children suffering for the sake of a few dollars. His life had been sheltered in some ways from the harsh realities some people have to live with. At first he didn't believe that children went blind when just a few dollars would have saved their eyesight. The contrasting images shocked him and made him realise how futile his life was. He may be a huge success but in his words, 'My life is a waste of time and that is why I am so unhappy.'

Afterwards he enthused, realising that his soul's purpose was to help children, 'Wow, there is so much more for me to do – I had better get busy. I am meant to be doing charity work and helping disadvantaged kids. I also need to hand over some of my money. I won't miss a few million here or there, so why not?' he smiled.

Now when I see him on television he has a relaxed calm air about him. And I'm pleased he's been able to find some inner peace – something that so many people in the public eye struggle to find.

New clients tell me all the time that they should be grateful for having a reasonable job but it feels like something is missing, or it doesn't feel quite right. No matter how hard they try, they will never be happy or fulfilled – just like my client the famous singer. With The Gallery and the spiritual techniques in this chapter, I help them find just what it is they are meant to be doing: their soul's purpose.

Another method I use with clients is the Soul Wisdom exercise. I suggest you do this regularly to connect with a higher energy. Soul wisdom will help you to know where you are heading and why. As you have been doing throughout this book, I suggest making notes on what you discover in your journal to refer to at a later date (see page 28).

Soul Wisdom

Find yourself a comfy place and relax.

◆ Carry out the Opening Up technique, as outlined on page 42, to begin.

◆ Allow your breathing to become long and deep as you go within and focus on the essence that is you.

◆ As you breathe you will become more of your own energy, the energy that makes up your life force. Somewhere inside you is a tiny spark that is your life force. It is the real you – the you that has existed from one lifetime to the next.

◆ Feel the energy in your body and notice it in your hands and feet, in your solar plexus and running through your spine. Be aware of your energy flowing from the top of your head right down to the tips of your toes. This is your life-force energy that exists in every cell of your body. This energy is the real you, not your flesh and bones which just make up your physical carriage this time round. Notice how your life force vibrates and glows as you become aware of your energy.

◆ Feel the energy rise up and up and right out of your body, floating a few inches above your head. Look down and feel free, feel weightless and unencumbered. You are complete and connected to the universal energy.

◆ You are pure energy, pure consciousness; a small ball of light and energy. This is the real you. The essence of you that feels peace, that loves all things and all people and sends love out to the world and the universe.

◆ Notice how simple and straightforward everything feels. Notice how clear your thought processes are. It is so obvious jut what is important and what isn't. You are a soul, a being of light so subtle, so powerful, so wise. You are immortal.

◆ Be aware of all the wisdom you have gained throughout the ages from you past and current lives. Keep that wisdom with you, and know that you can tap into it anytime you wish. Your spiritual energy can leave your body in this way whenever you want it to and each time you do so it will connect with the universal life force, wisdom and love. You will be at peace and know everything that you need to know. But best of all, you will know that really you need nothing because you have it all already.

◆ Now it is time to allow your soul to float back down and reconnect with your body. Float gently down and as you slide gently back into your body, know that in future you will be connected to the universal energy at all times. You are connected, you are energy. You are.

◆ Carry out the Closing Down exercise, as outlined on page 44, to finish.

....

We are all here to fulfill different things. You are not a soul that is just living this life for no reason. You have expanded across time – you have been here before and you will be here again – and if not, you will be somewhere else. This is because you are made from pure energy and energy can never disappear. Energy simply changes form. Just as water becomes steam, then becomes water again, then becomes ice, so you are an ever-changing being of light. All energy transforms, and you transform, too.

Once you discover the real essence of your self, the light being that is you, you will never again worry about what shoes you are wearing or if someone likes you or not. You will not worry about your boss's moods or your partner's honesty. You will rise above these thoughts, because in the blink of an eye this life will be gone and you will once again be part of the universal energy. You will be deciding who and where to be next, who you want around you, what you want to achieve and the lessons you need to learn. Hopefully, by breaking the negative associations with your past you will be ready to embrace your future in this reality and beyond.

Knowing your Past Lives

People have asked me why we are not born knowing about our past lives. If there are things we need to learn and overcome, why isn't this knowledge with us naturally?

The reason is because this knowledge would block our path even more. In the past we have not been evolved enough to process such information, so we have learnt through life experience – from events, from other people, from our own actions and their consequences. Now we are living in a time of great transformation. Things that would have taken many lifetimes to learn we can now understand in the blink of an eye. As souls, we are ready to connect with our true purpose. We are ready to leave behind day-to-day thoughts, wants and needs. We are ready to step into our true purpose. We are ready to be led along our journey by connecting with information usually only given to us when we are in spirit form.

The fact that you are reading this book and using these exercises means that you are ready to take the final step towards discovering your soul purpose. You are ready to wipe the slate clean and release anything that has plagued you, stopped you or slowed your progress. By clearing your path ahead, you can walk forward free and focused on the road ahead, wherever it may lead you.

Discovering your soul's purpose helps you to evolve. The more you evolve, the easier life becomes. You gain clarity and conviction about who you are, what you are doing and where you are heading. And I hope that by reading this book you have learnt about your past and your future, and answered some of your own important questions.

In the next chapter you will discover what the human race will be like in one hundred years' time. You will connect with the future, more highly evolved 'you', giving you a missing piece of the jigsaw to the eternal 'you'.

CHAPTER 8

The Future You — The Human Race A Century On

As well as spending years listening to my clients' fascinating tales of their future lives and exploring my own, I've also used Future Life Progression myself to see how the human race develops: socially, physically and spiritually. During my time-hopping jaunts I saw something strange – I found not one type of human species but two, which I call the 'Trans People' and the 'Grunters'. The human race literally splits into two. Trans People are highly evolved, whereas Grunters are less spiritually aware and live for the moment, with no wish to evolve.

At first I dismissed what I saw during my sessions because the information seemed strange and too fantastical, but over time my visions became stronger, clearer and more detailed – a sure sign they were accurate. I began writing down my findings and although I was confident of my visions, I was reassured in late 2006 to hear that a scientist had verified my information in a study. He predicts that the human race will split into two species (more on this later in this chapter). During FLP sessions with clients, and again in my solo sessions, I also discovered that some souls would evolve way beyond human life into what I call Light Beings, or souls that are evolved beyond human form.

Lydia is a good example of someone whose soul has

progressed rapidly. She came to me for Future Life Progression because she wanted to see if she would be rich in the future of her current life. When I explained to her that we could also see her next lifetime she said, 'Cool, let's hope I've found a wealthy hubby.'

Lydia is a lovely girl but by her own admission she cares little for anything other than the latest clothes. She told me, 'I want to do something but I can't be bothered to study and work hard, besides I'm not that clever.'

We looked at her life in five and ten years' time using The Lift, a method you will learn in a moment. She had married a nice chap who was comfortable and they had two children. Lydia was happy with the outcome. However, I was curious to see how she would be in a future soul experience so with her permission I took Lydia 100 years head. I was in for a surprise.

'Where are you?' I asked her.

'I am in a laboratory. I am very busy. My work is important.'

Her whole persona was totally different. The fickleness was replaced by a serious, almost stern attitude.

'What is your work?'

'I'm here to check the progress of a fluid I have scientists working on. This fluid could change the health of children. It's like a shot but it stops children suffering certain illnesses. I am determined to get this ready as soon as possible. They seem to have no sense of urgency, as their cosy lives have not taught them about hardship. That is what they need to experience.'

'Have you learned about hardship?' I asked.

'Yes.'

'When and what happened?'

'I went through spontaneous regression early in this life. I saw my previous lifetimes and I knew so little and experienced even

The Future You – The Human Race A Century On 197

less until one of my children got sick in my last incarnation. For several years I struggled to find a cure and eventually I did. It changed my whole view. I realised what was important and I have brought this into my current lifetime.'

She continued, 'I know I am being hard on the people in the lab. They do work long hours and care about people. But I almost expect them to work around the clock because this is so important.'

Lydia's story is no exception – I can't think of one person who I've seen as a client whose future self has not dramatically progressed by their next lifetime. I've given a lot of thought to why I've seen this spiritual progression time and again, and I've come to the simple conclusion that the type of people who I see in my office, and who come to my workshop, and you now reading this book, are on a spiritual quest. You want to know why you are here, how you can have a good life without hurting people and how you can best use your god-given gifts. Like a small child practising throwing and catching a ball, you are getting better and better at linking in with the spiritual power of the universe. By your next lifetime you will be able to throw the ball so high you won't be able to see it! I'm privileged because I am able to help people see their future evolved selves.

You can use the following exercise, The Lift, to travel forward and discover your future self and see how far you have progressed on your spiritual quest. One of the great benefits I have found with Future Life Progression is to be able to talk to my future self, and I am sure you will find the same. By talking to the future, more evolved, you, you will be able to tap into your own future wisdom – and solve problems.

Let me explain this another way. Imagine travelling back in time five years, then think about how much more you know

now, how wiser you now are and how you are so much more aware. Now think of something that was a problem to you then, maybe a difficult work colleague or a relationship problem. Perhaps you were wondering whether to move home, book a holiday or even whether to trust someone.

Now think about how you could advise yourself by steering your past self in the right direction.

You can do the same by tapping into your future self, the you who has moved beyond current problem and its limitations, unhindered by the emotions and worries that go with it. This gives you a clear perspective because you now have something that everyone wants – hindsight.

The Lift

◆ Carry out the Opening Up technique, as outlined on page 42, to begin.

◆ Imagine you are at the base of a vast mountain. Look up and see the peak high in the clouds and notice a long and winding path leading to the top.

◆ Take a deep breath and step onto the path and follow it round and up the mountain. As you take each step, feel yourself relaxing. Soon you are so calm you feel as if you do not have a care in the world.

◆ Keep to the path and notice that the air is becoming cooler as you slowly make you way up the mountain. Breathe in the clean mountain air and look around – you can see a long way into the distance. You look out over fields and hills. You look up at the clouds floating across a clear blue sky.

◆ Up and up you stroll getting nearer and nearer to the peak, and before long you are there. You have made it to the top and you feel proud of yourself for getting this far. You can now see for miles and as you look to the horizon, you feel in touch with the beauty of the world you live in.

◆ Suddenly you notice a door in the side of the mountain a short way down the path. You walk down and notice the door is wooden and shabby. It looks very old and worn. Reach out to the rusty handle and pull the door open. Inside is a dark cave. It takes a few moments for your eyes to adjust, but before long you notice another door across the cave.

◆ Walk up to the door and realise that it is a lift. You open the door and inside is a black leather comfy chair. You sink into the soft leather chair and see a remote control on the arm. On the remote control you see the words. 'Future Lifetime of…' then your own name. Beneath the words is a white button.

◆ Make yourself comfortable in the chair, then press the white button. The door slides shut and you hear a whirring noise as the lift begins to move upwards. You wonder where the lift can be going – you are already so close to the top of the mountain, but up and up it rises. You realise that this lift is really a portal capable of taking you far into the future.

◆ Suddenly the lift banks to the right and zooms further upwards at a right angle. And you know that you are moving forward in time. You also know that time is passing very quickly.

◆ A voice says, 'You are arriving at your destination.' The lift stops and you stand up ready to walk through the door where you will enter your future lifetime. Once through the door, you will be aware of the future you.

◆ The door slides open. Walk through the door and step outside. Where are you? Do you feel male or female? Do you feel light or heavy? Become aware of your surroundings. What do you feel your role is?

◆ Be aware of the future you. Be aware of how you feel and of your wisdom. Be aware of how evolved you are. In your mind, ask the future you for any advice they have for you right now. The future you has the benefit of hindsight.

◆ Take whatever answer is given to you then step back inside the lift and watch the door slide shut. As the lift descends back to your current time, focus on the message you have just been given and how it can help you in your current time.

◆ The lift arrives back at the top of the mountain. Walk across the cave and back through the old wooden door.

◆ Walk back down the mountain and feel at peace. You have just connected to your future self and now anytime you wish you can go back and gain wisdom from the future you.

◆ Carry out the Closing Down technique, as outlined on page 44, to finish.

So now that you know how to connect with your own future self, I want to tell you about the future of the human race as a whole. Remember, we are all interconnected and part of a bigger picture.

The Future of the Human Race

Firstly, from my own forays into the future I've discovered that the human race finally grows up, and it doesn't take long for it to happen. In fact, by our next lifetime many of you will have evolved rapidly, and in some cases several thousand years' worth of evolution.

My own findings have been backed up by the constant information I've received whilst progressing hundreds of people into their next lifetime, which is usually any time between 50 and 500 years. I've seen, in every case, that their future selves are far more evolved than would be expected by their next lifetime.

Let's break this concept down into little chunks. Think about how people were in your granny's day. What were their morals and values? What were their opinions on war, relationships and money? Attitudes do change over the years, but not usually as much as you may expect.

Consider the smaller issues, too. Think about your parent's attitude to buying gifts. Were they extravagant? Prudent? Now ponder your attitude to buying presents. How much different is it to your parents'? Think about their rules on love, sex, work and friendship. Compare their opinions to your opinions now and you may find you are more like them that you realised.

The point I'm trying to make is that over a generation or two the views and attitudes of people don't alter that much. You may feel you are more liberal than your parents, as is often the case, but if you begin to examine yourself you will find that your attitudes overall won't have changed much. Yet my clients showed me over and over again that by their next lifetimes, which can be as little as 80 years away, the human race is very different.

Attitudes, morals and views have changed radically, and the amazing thing is that every single one of the hundreds of people I've progressed has evolved far more than expected.

The Trans People

For several years, as in Lydia's Future Life Progression, I witnessed the same pattern in sessions over and over again as clients jumped ahead in their soul's evolution – and recounted lives as totally different beings. I have given these beings, our future selves, a name – I can them Trans People. 'Trans' is a Latin word meaning 'across', 'beyond' or 'opposite'.

Trans and Emotions

♦ The first thing I noticed about Trans People was that they are a lot less needy about relationships. I have many clients who are almost frantic about their love lives – they fret about who they are seeing, how it's going and if the relationship will last. Who hasn't at some point worried about a relationship? Even my clients who worried the most have a different mindset in their future lives. If I ask them, 'Do you have a husband or wife? They reply with indifference that if they have it's fine, or if they don't it's also fine. The same applies to money, the second most emotive subject clients bring to me. If I ask them if they're well off or poor, they don't understand the question. They react in much the same way you would if I asked you if you had plenty of cheese in your fridge. They wonder why I was asking such an odd question. I'm not talking about the odd isolated case here; this was during each and every progression.

♦ I've discovered that Trans People are content whether they are in a relationship or not. They view life and people as a greater whole. They are often connected to groups of people. They are more aware of how everyone feels as opposed to individuals or simply themselves. Work appears to be more important than relationships with many doing jobs that they feel are vitally important to the world and the human race.

♦ They love people and feel more connected to them as a whole. They feel love for everyone. There is great strength in this universal connection. Instead of everything resting emotionally on one person, who may leave us or die, by being connected to a greater whole we have more stability. It also means that everyone looks after each other as opposed to just their own little unit – or just themselves. In our current time we are very separate from one another, even those we love. Somehow in the future, and I've seen this repeatedly in client's next lifetimes, we will learn to connect more with people in general. We realise that when we talk about collective consciousness, it is total – we are connected to everyone and everything. If you hurt another person, you hurt yourself. This is the true meaning of karma, or cause and effect. Remember the old saying, 'divide and conquer'? Being connected to everyone creates strength from unity.

♦ Trans People are not needy when it comes to love and emotions. They are not so dependent on one person to make their life happy. Trans People are more sensual. They are extremely sensitive and thus gain greater pleasure from intimacy. By having a connection to someone they will feel their energy from a long distance. If someone they have a special connection with enters a room they will feel it in their energy field. If their energy no longer connects with that of another they can move on with less emotional upset.

Case Study

Pippa had been a client of mine for many years, and boy did she keep me busy as she lurched from one bad relationship to another. Things would start off well, but within a short space of time she would become more and more needy, and on each occasion this began earlier in the relationship, resulting in the poor man running for his life.

As each new relationship hit the rocks I would receive frantic phone calls pleading for a same-day appointment. Over the years, I've advised Pippa to be calm and take relationships one day at a time and I have also suggested various therapists, but nothing seemed to help. Within days of meeting someone she would become demanding, constantly phone them and even turn up on their doorstep uninvited – to be frank, she came across as a bit of a bunny boiler.

When I started using FLP I realised it might be able to help her, but I wasn't sure just how effective it would be. But as Pippa slipped into her future lifetime her whole persona changed and she became relaxed but strong.

She began talking at length about her work as a colour therapist where she takes her patients and soaks them in a bath of coloured liquid whilst shining coloured lights around the room.

Apparently the results will be incredible. Pippa never mentioned anything to do with relationships and so I asked her, 'Do you have a partner?'

'Yes, he is in the same line of work as me.'

'How is it going?'

'Very well, we are both busy people and he works away for long periods of time but that suits me because I have so much to do.'

This was far removed from the Pippa I knew and it was clear to me she was a Trans Person – she had the relaxed air of a Trans and was fully aware of her soul's purpose. She cared about others and was no longer needy. Her priorities were less about her and more about the world and the human race as a whole. It was wonderful to hear that she had finally found peace and happiness in her personal life.

I asked Pippa to absorb the happy and relaxed feeling and to bring it back with her to her current time.

After the session I didn't hear from Pippa for some time. However, I did see a mutual friend who told me that she had met a lovely man and they were planning to move in together, which I thought was fantastic news.

Trans and Their Looks

◆ Sci-fi movies have led us to believe that we will all dress the same in the future, usually by wearing some sort of silver boiler suit. Yet our future selves will want to feel individual just as much as we do today. Just because we are more connected to others doesn't mean we want to look like clones. Trans wear simple, comfortable, well-designed, well-cut, lightweight clothing in plain colours.

◆ Our future selves are lighter in weight and taller, spindly but lean and strong. Trans are good-looking people. This has come about by good-looking, fit and healthy people marrying, a kind of positive in-breeding if you like. They have big eyes, clear skin and high cheekbones.

Trans and the Concept of Nationality

As I worked with my clients I became more and more intrigued. I began by asking them questions such as: Where do you live? What country are you from? Have you a partner? What work do you do? These were obvious questions to me and so I found it difficult to understand why my clients seemed to not understand.

One question that seemed to particularly flummox my clients was, 'What nationality are you?' They found the question irrelevant and couldn't understand why I would want to know such a thing. Nationality, the concept of a separate identity, wasn't important to them.

Case Study

Jenny is a good example of a Trans Person and their concept of nationality. When we used The Lift technique (see page 198) she found herself 150 years in the future, working in a remote scientific outstation with a dozen or so people. I asked her where she was from. 'What do you mean?' she asked.

'Where do you live?' I prompted her.

'Here at the station,' she told me.

'But it is a remote outstation, do people live their all their lives and bring up families there?'

'No of course not,' she said calmly.

'So where did you grow up?'

'In America.'

'And where do you go when you are on leave?'

'America, Kansas.'

'So that is where you live?'

'No I live at the station, I just visit Kansas.'

I found it odd to think that the place where she grew up was not thought of as 'home', as her identity. If you were to ask a teacher with a teaching post overseas, or a soldier stationed abroad, they would not call their place of work their home.

I then asked Jenny, 'So what are the nationalities of the people you work with?'

I was curious to see if the research station was a group effort of a number of countries, and maybe discover which countries worked together or had formed coalitions.

'What do you mean?' she asked me for a second time.

'The people you work with – where are they from?'

'They are from the station.'

'But where did they grow up?'

'I don't know.'

'Has the subject never come up?

'No.'

'Do you never talk about childhood things, school, families?' I pressed her.

'No, why would we?'

'So what do you talk about?'

Jenny began to sound irritated by my questions, 'We talk about work, what we are working on and how we can improve it. We do not talk about things that aren't to do with work.'

'Even when you have finished work? Don't you sometimes just sit and relax and chat about things?'

'Yes, but we talk about what still needs to be done. Look, this project is vitally important to plant life and if we can achieve our aims we will greatly enhance the quality of our plants and food sources. We will be making the world healthier, so why would be want to talk about things long since past? I don't understand why you're so interested in the past.'

Jenny's thoughts sum up the general attitude of Trans people, in that they are concerned with the bigger picture and making the world a better place. They are not concerned with creating concepts of 'separateness', i.e. things which set them apart from others. In a way, they are an example of a 'global' community.

Time and again I've had similar conversations in FLP sessions whilst clients have been in a deeply relaxed state. To our future selves, where someone is from is irrelevant. In fact people don't know where other people originated from and they're not in the slightest bit interested. At first this bothered me because I find it fascinating to meet people from other cultures. By the sound of some of the experiences my clients were having, it appeared that we would all be quite cold and dull. But I soon began to realise that because the Trans People were evolved, their priorities were different. They were excited by other things. They were more interested in the greater whole and how they could make the world a better place. This concept to them was far more interesting than cultural differences.

Also, in preceding years people moved countries so much that the boundaries separating countries, mentally and physically, have become blurred. Again if you think back to granny's day it was rare to eat foreign food in the UK. But today a world cuisine, from Thai to Italian, is a normal part of our weekly diet, and by the same token cultures in the future will blur over time.

Trans and Music

Over time, I pondered if this evolved group ever relaxed – they seemed so serious and lacking in humour. As I asked them about their leisure time, music came up over and over, and it will become a far more important part of our lives than even today.

♦ Trans are aware that music affects their energy points, especially their chakras, and because their sensitivity is heightened they're aware of hundreds of chakras. We are aware to a certain extent of music affecting us; at times we can be moved to tears by hearing a beautiful piece of music. We can also cringe at certain sounds– think of the expression, 'Her voice went straight through me' or someone scraping their fingernails down a blackboard. Music can soothe or agitate, it can excite or depress. Trans have discovered much, much more about the power of noise vibration.

♦ They are aware of how music affects the energy points and so they choose music to create how they want to feel. There is music to bring about a feeling of productivity, relaxation, to lessen pain, to enhance feelings of love, to aid concentration and learning ability. They can also use it to heighten their intuition, sexuality, creativity and even physical strength.

♦ I began taking jumps into the future myself to discover more about the Trans use of sound. I discovered the music for productivity sounded rather like some German music (think of the German band Kraftwerk who in the 1970s began to produce industrial sounding electronic music which was 20 years ahead of its time, and still sounds fresh now) which made sense to me because the German people always have been an industrious and productive nation.

◆ Peaceful music was similar to the string sounds often heard in Chinese or Japanese music, only far more subtle. It was almost like thousands of violins, with some ranging from pitches you can barely hear. As I focused on the sound I could feel a shimmer of energy flow through me. It felt emotional yet peaceful and could so easily move you to tears.

◆ I discovered that the use of music had moved up a level. I saw an image of musical technicians experimenting on groups of people. They would try slight variations of sounds and vibration until they produced the effect they most wanted to achieve. Music was used to bring out emotions in people with problems, and for making felons aware of their crimes. This was achieved during their police interview by playing music that would stir emotions deep within them. Sometimes it would make them aware of why they committed crimes, but it also brought empathy to the surface and made them realise, and experience, how their crimes hurt others.

◆ Trans people don't just listen to music, they can also feel it. They're more aware of the vibrations and their effects. They know that music produces different states within us. Some of the sounds I heard quite surprised me – they seem to enjoy a techno type of music, which grounds them by stimulating their base chakra.

Good Vibrations

Chris Ellis, a sound engineer, says, 'Sound resonates and vibrates on any animate and inanimate object. By the use of specific frequencies tuned to the vibration of that particular thing, sound can fundamentally change its make-up, structure, and emotional and physical state. In short, I could create a noise or frequency that could make a person feel euphoric, depressed or even experience an urge to go to the toilet. The idea that sound and its frequencies could be explored and utilised in the future is possible. However, I think it will be many years before using such methods become mainstream.'

The Grunters

My client's fascinating stories about their future lives whetted my appetite and, keen to learn more, I continued to make journeys into the future myself to see what I could discover about the development of the human race. But then something strange happened again. After some years of peeking at the future of homo sapiens, I realised that not everyone evolves. I found a subspecies, one that my clients hadn't mentioned – and I couldn't work out why. I've called the people of this subspecies the 'Grunters' from the old English word 'grunnettan' which means 'a person or animal that makes a loud noise'.

At first I dismissed my findings and the existence of this subspecies – after all, my clients hadn't mentioned them. But

time again they appeared in my visions. Although I was confident of what I'd seen, I was reassured when Dr Oliver Curry, a
scientist from the Darwin research centre at the London School
of Economics, verified my findings with a study that was made
public at the end of 2006.

I used a recording of my own voice talking me through the
process of FLP to guide myself into the future – so in reality, I
put myself into a trance! I wanted to experience FLP just as my
clients did, and I discovered a little more about the Grunters –
people who live for the moment and are less spiritually aware.
Those who are interested in FLP and other spiritual matters
will not be Grunters in their future lifetimes, they will be the
Trans who you've already met. Anyone who has a session of
FLP, reads any kind of book on self-development or takes a
course means that they're very spiritually aware and wanting to
grow. Grunters have no interest in evolving or growing as
people and this is why I hadn't met them through any of my
clients; their souls simply did not incarnate in the future into
the species of Grunters.

The Two Tribes

Evolutionary theorist Dr Oliver Curry believes the human race
will split into two new subspecies within the next thousand
years. One will be a genetic upper class who will be tall, slim,
healthy, symmetrical, intelligent and creative. The underclass
will be squat, ugly, dim-witted, asymmetrical and unhealthy.

This, he believes, is a result of people becoming choosier
about their sexual partners and causing humanity to divide into
subspecies. He named the two species as 'gracile' for the upper

class (what I call Trans People) and robust for the lower class (the Grunters).

Dr Curry said, 'The Bravo Evolution Report suggests that the future of man will be a story of the good, the bad and the ugly. While science and technology have the potential to create an ideal habitat for the next millennium, there is the possibility of a monumental genetic hangover in the subsequent millennia due to an over-reliance on technology reducing our natural capacity to resist disease, or our evolved ability to get along with each other. After that, things could get ugly, with the possible mergence of genetic "haves" and "have nots".'

Light Beings

Throughout history and legend, there are stories of spiritual helpers appearing in a number of forms. The Bible describes beings and angels visiting humans and helping their progress. The Old Testament mentions 'an angel of the lord' and there are many mentions of angelic beings in the New Testament. The word angel means 'messenger' in Hebrew and Greek.

There are a wealth of stories circulating now, in books and the mainstream press, from people who believe they have been visited by an angelic being. They usually describe them as translucent, or shimmering, which is exactly how my clients who find themselves as future Light Beings describe themselves. Could some of the many sightings of ghosts and angels actually be our future selves travelling back in time to aid our current selves?

Eminent future life progressionist Dr Bruce Goldberg believes so. In fact, he also believes that many alien abductions are our very own species travelling back through time and attempting to help us evolve. These time travellers, which he calls 'chrononauts', he claims come from between 1,000 and 3,000 years in our future and have mastered teleportation. The first time travellers arrive by a type of flying saucer and they are from 1,000 to 1,500 years in the future. In his book *Past Lives, Future Lives Revealed*, Goldberg says these time travellers are with us now: 'The time traveller's main purpose in visiting us is not to abduct 20th-century humans for genetic study. It is to accelerate our spiritual development so that we (they in the future) can ascend to join God.'

During their FLP sessions, many of my clients found themselves in a form they were unable to understand. The bafflement in the voices of my subjects told me they'd no idea what they were. Although they are interested in tarot, FLP and such like, many of them have little esoteric knowledge and know nothing about Light Beings. I would ask my usual key questions over and over again, and the replies that came back told me they were not in human form. To my question, 'Are you male or female?' they would reply:

'I'm not sure, neither.'

'This is really odd but I just seem to be a ball of light.'

'I don't know what to make of this but I am sort of translucent.'

And even, 'I am really light and floaty, almost like a fairy.'

I would then ask another key question: 'Where are you, inside or outside?'

They would answer, 'Neither. I am just nowhere. I am floating but I am not sure where I am.'

I began to realise that although Trans People are much more progressed than us, some souls that evolve are even more advanced. I call these souls Light Beings.

In an early session of FLP, I took myself forward and I, too, was unsure as to who or what I was when I linked in with my future self. At first I thought I was on an aeroplane but I soon realised I was on a craft that was about to land vertically on some sort of landing base. My first thoughts were, 'Oh boy, this isn't Earth.'

The part of me that was arriving on this planet was totally uninterested in what was happening. The other part of me still in the here-and-now was fascinated. The landing was as easy as parking a car, or if you are like me, easier. The craft gently glided down. No one looked out of the window or paid any attention. There were a couple of people on the landing base, but this seemed all very routine to everyone. Think about how you are when travelling by bus and you will have an idea of how my future self reacted to arriving on some far-off planet – it was run of the mill.

I felt lighter and somehow at one with my environment. Now I can see that I was a Light Being but at the time I had no idea what or who I was and it was confusing. All I knew was that it felt so right. It was as if I was connected to everything and everybody, and this in turn made me feel strong and secure.

My current self seemed so primitive compared to what I had just experienced and I hoped I would bring a little of the future me back to the present. This is what inspired me to develop the technique to bring back a little of our future, more evolved, selves.

As I stepped off the craft I knew the place was familiar to me in that lifetime. I was immediately struck by the colours of this plane – I noticed that everything was pastel coloured, absolutely everything. I was conscious of myself in my current life and from this perception the colours I live with every day seemed so garish. The trees outside my window were so very, very green. The sky seemed so very, very blue. My future self flinched and thought, 'How can you live with those colours?' They seemed far too strong. I then became aware that my body was so much lighter. I was almost floating, I felt lighter and easier.

Again I became aware of my current self and the heaviness of my current body. I smiled at how heavy my clothes were. They were like a suit of armour. As I looked back at my current self it all seemed so primitive and a million miles from how far I'd come in my future life.

Light Beings in my Office

During a session of FLP in my office, Ed had a similar experience to me. In his current life he had given up his car sales business after taking a course in self-development. He had discovered a whole new world, and he set about finding out even more. He studied NLP (neurolinguistic programming) and hypnotherapy, then studied with a shaman. Today, he is a leading self-development trainer. When he came to see me he wanted to know where he was heading in his current life, but was also curious about his future lifetime. What he learnt during his hour-long session left him dazed for several days.

He told me, 'I am in some sort of a temple, but there is no floor. It seems to be floating through space. This is so odd.'

'Are you male or female?'

'I am formless. I seem to be made of energy.'

'Are you alone?'

'No, there are others like me here.'

'Who are they?'

'Not sure – we seem to communicate but we do not talk. We are telepathic.'

'Do you have a role?'

'Yes, I teach and guide.'

'Where do you do this?'

'From here I can reach many people but I also travel. Wow, I can change form. I can become more solid when I need to. It depends on who I am teaching.'

Ed described shape-shifting into forms as he arrived on certain planets. He would never appear totally solid, but could become partially solid if need be to connect with those he was teaching. The Light Beings of the future tend to teach or assist not just our species, but also others. They are usually already working in a spiritual field or are highly developed in their current lifetime – healers, psychics or advanced practitioners of meditation.

Josey is a pretty down-to-earth girl. In her progressions of five and ten years into her future she saw things that you would expect, such as a husband and baby and career developments. Her future lifetime proved to be startlingly different, however – she saw herself as a Light Being.

'Are you male or female?' I asked her.

'Female,' she told me.

'What age?'

'I'm 33 in your time.'

'What are you wearing?'

'White cloth, a long white tunic.'

'What is your hair like?'

She replied, 'Free. Just free. It is dark – dark hair'

'Are you wearing any shoes?'

'No. I have bare feet.'

'What is your role?' I asked.

'People come to me. I help them.'

'How?'

'I guide them.'

'Where do you live?'

'I have many homes.'

'Where are they?'

She replied, surprised, 'A home is a home. It is somewhere where you can be free and find solitude. It is where people look after me. They care for me.'

'What food do you eat?'

'I don't eat food,' said Josey.

'What do you live on?' I asked, keeping my tone neutral despite my surprise.

'Light. I feed off the light.'

'How?'

'It gives us peace and growth and energy.'

'What can you see outside?'

'Light,' she said immediately.

'Are there any plants or trees outside?'

Looking confused, she told me, 'They are inside.'

'What is the outside temperature?'

'It's cold. It's always cold. I have never seen a warm day,' she says.

'Do you ever go outside?'

'Sometimes.'

'What do you wear when you go outside?' I asked.

'The same as inside. Our tunics are made of synthetic fibres that have a natural thermostat – they keep us cool in the warm and warm in the cold. They are multi-seasonal.'

Case Study

The first time I met Rohini, I was struck by how she was different from other girls of her age – she had awareness and wisdom beyond her years. She spoke passionately about her work as a scientist conducting clinical drug trials into medicines, including everything from high blood pressure to diabetes.

When she came to see me, Rohini was developing new vaccines, but deep down she wanted to work with natural remedies and holistic medicine. I suggested a past life session for her – I had read her cards a few times and I was curious to know about her previous existence to see if this would help her move forward in this life. Rohini is sweet, very feminine and extremely polite, so I was quite surprised when during the PLR her voice became deeper and sterner.

'We are in dense jungle. The heat is intense but I don't care,' she told me.

'Are you male or female?'

'Male.'

'What do you look like?'

'I am dark. I have long hair and a moustache. My name is Alfredo.'

'You said "we"; who is with you?' I nudged her.

'Him,' Rohini sneered, 'he doesn't want to be here. I feel quite aggressive towards him. He is tagging along but I am forcing him. He wants a peaceful life.'

'What is he like?'

'He is a little boy. I make him carry the ammunition.'

'Where are you?'

'Columbia, in the jungle.'

'What are you doing?'

'Our family are drug barons.'

'Who is the boy?'

'He is my son. I do not love him,' Rohini made this statement without emotion. She continued, 'He feels like a burden. I want him to be like me – a man. He is weak. I hit him.'

'Why do you hit him?'

'I can't do my job because he is there. When I hit him he just looks at me'

I asked Rohini what they were doing in the jungle. She replied, 'We must keep a look out people for who want to take things from us.'

'What do you have that they may want?'

'Drugs – we have lots of drugs. It is my job to deliver them but he slows me down. There are dangerous people here that would kill me as soon as look at me and he just slows me down. He just wants to help people,' she spat.

Listening to Rohini seemed a million miles from the polite young lady sat with her eyes closed in my office. I asked Rohini to move forward to her latter years. Her voice became slow and weaker. She said, 'We are sitting under a tree. He is older now; he is big built, very big.'

'Who?'

'My son. He is good. I am frail but I can see the goodness in him. He wants things to change.'

'In what way?'

'He wants to stop the drugs. He is good to people. I respect him.'

There was sadness in her voice I asked, 'How is your relationship with him?'

'He respects me but he doesn't love me.'

'What is the lesson for you from this lifetime?'

'I hear a voice telling me not to suppress my feelings. It is weak to do so.

I should respect and love people before it is too late.'

Rohini had obviously evolved a great deal in her current lifetime. She had grown beyond using drugs for the wrong reasons to working with them for good use. She has helped many people by making sure new medical drugs are safe to use.

After her PLR, I was curious to see just how far she would evolve in her future lifetime, so I suggested a session of FLP. Many people who do good work in this lifetime are very highly progressed spiritually in their next existence. The most highly evolved are Light Beings and I was not too surprised to discover that Rohini had progressed to this level when I took her forward.

'Are you a man or a woman?'

'Woman.'

'How old are you?'

'I am very young.'

'Where are you?'

'I am standing on a podium. I am lecturing, but it is out in the open. I am dressed in white with bare feet. Everyone is dressed in white.'

'What are you lecturing about?'

'The conversation is soothing and loving and about communication, but I am not speaking.'

'What do you mean?'

'We do not need to communicate by talking. We use our minds.'

'Who are the audience?'

'They are men and women. They are older, they are on a pilgrimage. They have done their life's work. Now, this is their time for their own development.'

'What is happening?'

'We are using telepathy. I don't need to guide people. I am more of a host. Everything here is so perfect.'

'Where is this?'

'Not Earth. It is similar to Earth but has higher vibration, a different energy. On Earth there are buildings. It is very green on Earth. It has more colour. It's brighter, the colours are more garish than here. The colours seem almost aggressive they are so harsh. This planet is whiter – it has a different type of light. Not like sunlight.'

'Do the people live there, or have they travelled there?'

'They have travelled there. I feel as if I am like an angel. I am just assisting them – they already know what they are doing.'

As soon as Rohini said she felt as if she was like an angel I knew that she was a Light Being and I asked her the key question, 'Do you feel heavy or light, or just normal weight?'

'I am like a human body but it is like I am floating.'

As we saw earlier this is a classic sign of someone who has evolved into a Light Being. I asked Rohini how far she had travelled into the future. She told me,

'Three hundred years.'

'You appear to have evolved a great deal from your present incarnation. Why is that?'

'Being close to God brings me close to the energy field. It is a 'knowing'. It is a bond with God.'

I threw in another key question. 'Where do you live?'

Rohini replied, 'I do not understand the question.'

Every time I have asked this question of a Light Being they have not understood the concept. Light beings don't live anywhere. They just are. They exist in energy form and because they aren't solid, they don't need solid things around them.

Next I asked Rohini, 'Do you need anything?'

'I need to be close to the sun. I worship the sun. It helps me to connect more. The energy of the sun helps me when I have a lot of work to do.'

'How does the sun help you to work?'

'My energy source is the sun.'

'Do you have work other than lecturing?'

'Yes, I visit other planets, including Earth.'

'What do you do there?'

'I prevent car accidents in the dimension and time you exist in now. I touch people on the shoulder when they fall asleep at the wheel. I know when something is going to happen. I like doing this, but I do not like the Earth connection.'

'What do you mean?' I wanted to know.

'I like to see the green of earth but it is not home. There is too much pain.'

Rohini spoke with great authority and it seemed she also had the ability to travel back in time and help people on Earth. She is a wonderful example of someone who has evolved very quickly, and she is now in touch with her soul path and feels incredibly happy and inspired by her discovery of her future self.

Imagine if this process, Future Life Progression, could affect the many people who lead bad lives now? Would they have a huge turnaround, like Rohini in their current life or in the future? I like to think that many of them would – perhaps the Home

Office should make past life and future life therapy compulsory for all prison inmates! It might help people to break out of their cycles of bringing destruction and unhappiness upon themselves and others.

Your Future Self Can Help you Now

Rohini, Josey, Ed and the other Light Beings I met in my office during sessions often gave consistent answers to the same questions, which I found amazing. They talked of travelling through time, helping others and living on pure energy. It makes sense to me that if we can progress into the future then our future selves can travel back. And if you could travel back in time and help yourself you surely would, wouldn't you?

It also makes sense to me that knowledge we gain in our future lifetime can be brought back to help us now. Jude did just that – during a session she saw herself sending vast and brilliant energy to trouble-spots, places that had problems. She described a village in terror as the occupants attempted to escape the dangers of war that had forced them from their homes into the mountains. Jude could see the energy flow from her and light up a cave that the villagers were hiding in.

Several weeks later Jude visited her daughter who was having a lot of problems with her wayward step daughter. Jude told me, 'The atmosphere in my daughter's house was awful. Her partner's daughter was very rude to her. The rows were not pretty and at times descend into more of a street brawl. This had been building up for weeks and was getting worse.'

Jude was desperate to make things better for them and she could see that things were about to become even worse. She felt quite nervous and decided to try and fill the house with the same energy she had witnessed in her future lifetime.

She told me later, 'I imagined light around myself, first to cleanse me in preparation, and then I sent the light around the whole room. Gradually I spread it into the entire house and eventually to the room at the bottom of the garden where the step daughter lived.'

As she sent the light to the girl's room Jude could see that the girl wasn't very happy. As the light reached the girl and swamped the room, Jude had a vision of her reaction. The girl began rushing around, throwing things across the room and making a lot of noise. She then felt the girl reacting and attempting to push back the light. As Jude witnessed this she sent even more brilliant waves of light into the room. She then left, not expecting this to have helped. She told her daughter, 'I have tried to send some good energy to the girl. I'm really sorry for you, but there's nothing I can do to help.'

The next day Jude returned expecting World War Three to be in progress. 'I couldn't believe my eyes. My daughter and her step daughter had made up as if nothing had ever happened – after months of worsening arguments. At first I thought it was coincidence, but then I realised this was the good feeling that was in my future regression that I'd passed on to the villagers as they tried to escape.'

Angels of the Future

Just imagine that if some of the many thousands of stories of angels guiding or rescuing people were actually our friends from the future popping back to give us a nudge. This seemed to be the case with Charlotte – I wasn't too surprised to find that she was a Light Being in her future lifetime, although after the session she looked at me blankly and said, 'A Light what?'

As I took her forward I could see her aura changing to become pure white.

'You have entered your future lifetime. What do you look like?' I asked.

'Mm, well I am like an angel.'

'In what way?'

'Well, it is as if I have a human body but like I am floating. I feel very light.'

'Where do you live?'

'I don't understand the question.'

'Do you have a place that is your base?' I asked again.

'My base is wherever I am.'

'Do you have a family?'

'No, but I am not lonely.'

'Do you need anything?'

'My energy source is the sun.'

'What is your role?'

'I have many roles. At the moment I am assisting people in their own development.'

'What people?'

'They are retired and now have time for themselves and their own growth. They know what to do; I just assist them. As a host.'

I then asked Charlotte what else she did because I was curious to know what her other roles were.

'I travel back in time and prevent car accidents,' she told me – which surprised me, as this is what Rohini had said too, only weeks before!

'How do you do that?' I asked, intrigued.

'I know when things are going to happen. I just send them the thought 'slow down' when they fall asleep at the wheel.'

Charlotte beamed with pride as she told me this. She explained that this was something extra she did. Almost as if guiding others and hosting their growth meetings was her day job and waking drivers was like being a special duty police officer in her spare time, only this copper travelled back through time to save many lives.

Light Beings - the Evidence

Many people who have had out of body experiences have encountered Light Beings. In 1958, a successful businessman Robert Monroe, from the Monroe Institute, began to find himself leaving his physical body to travel to other realms. During his travels he met Light Beings and he commented in his book, now a seminal text, *Journeys Out of the Body*, 'Whatever they may be, the beings have the ability to radiate warmth of friendliness that evokes complete trust.' He added, 'They are totally solicitous as to the well being of the human beings with whom they are associated.'

Michael Talbot in his book, *The Holographic Universe* asks, 'Who are the beings of light?' He answers his own question by saying, 'As for the ultimate identity of these beings, we can deduce from their behaviour that they are older, wiser, and possess some deep and loving connection to the human species. But beyond this, the question remains unanswered as to whether they are gods, angels, the souls of human beings who have finished reincarnating, or something that is altogether beyond human comprehension.'

By tapping into the future we can discover our world, our future selves and even bring a little of it back with us. In the next chapter we will be taking a panoramic view and I will reveal the results of my research into the future. If you think a lot has happened to the human race in a relatively short space of time, wait until you discover how the world as a whole is doing. I'll explore how we will travel, study, bring up our children and power our homes; which countries will thrive and which will slump. Think back to how much the world has changed in the last 100 years – technology, how we live, work and play has altered beyond belief. Then get ready, because the next century will be even more exciting than the last.

CHAPTER 9
The Future World

After working closely with so many clients, and my own regular journeys into the future, I was utterly hooked into the process of Future Life Progression. I regularly experienced visions of the future, about the people of our world and beyond. I was transfixed and wanted to know more about our environment, how we would live our lives and how society functioned. So, I began scanning the world: I took myself into a relaxed state and followed the FLP techniques I used with my clients. I looked down on the planet and then zoned into certain places. I had a long list of questions. Firstly, I wanted to discover which countries had thrived? Which had faltered? Were there any wars? How did we travel, power our vehicles and our homes? How would we educate our children and heal ourselves?

We are seeing great changes in the climate of the world even now – for example, the melting of the polar ice caps. I wanted to know if the environment would continue to change, and if so how drastically? Had pollution ruined our world? These were all burning questions that honestly worried me. I began to have regular sessions on my own so that I could gain a wider overview of the future of the planet. Yes, I had already discovered the Trans and Grunters, but I wanted to know more about how society was functioning, how the planet was coping and bigger issues. I realised that I needed to have a clear picture and so I chose to look 20, 50 and 100 years into the future.

Many people have asked me why I didn't choose 1,000 years, but, by discovering what's happening in just 20, 50 and 100 years, we can begin to guide ourselves in the right direction. What we do now affects the near future and we can work towards it. Besides, my glimpses of 1,000 years left me baffled because the technology was so far beyond anything that could be understood. All I know is that in 1,000 years we will be multidimensional, using and understanding energy in ways that are beyond us now.

The First-ever Future Life Progression Study

My journeys and my many FLP sessions with clients often gave me a wealth of information about the future, but I realised that the visions needed to be verified by people who were not influenced in any way. So I conducted a study. I put together a guided visualisation of 100 years in the future and I then held workshops at my offices with small groups. I also sent out CDs to volunteers. Some of the topics were the same, some different. This type of study has never been conducted before, to my knowledge, so not only is the process unique but the results are groundbreaking.

I had no idea how much interest there would be once I posted the request for participants on my website. I was overwhelmed to receive requests for the CD from all over the world, including Australia, New Zealand, Dubai, Switzerland, Spain, Ireland, America, Canada and Japan – as well as dozens of people in my home country of Britain.

None of the participants had any idea what the others had

seen in their journeys. They were each given a questionnaire to fill in – and the results were astonishing. If you would like to try this exercise, please do so before you read the study's findings – which follow after the study's FLP journey below, The World in 100 Years – so you will not be influenced by the results.

You can download the following exercise, The World in 100 Years, from my website www.futurelifeprogression.com where you can listen and follow the guided visualisation session live or download it onto your iPod, or MP3 player, free of charge. Alternatively, you can record yourself speaking the visualisation, or ask a friend to read it to you.

By the way, do send me your findings – email them to me at anne@futurelifeprogression.com. My website is constantly updated with new FLP experiences. Between us we can compile an extensive profile and find out what we need to know to make our world a better place.

The World in 100 Years

◆ Find yourself a comfy place and allow yourself to relax. You may wish to play soft background music.

◆ Carry out the Opening Up exercise (see page 42) to begin.

◆ Put all your current thoughts to one side and concentrate on your breathing. As you breathe, feel your abdomen rise and fall and with each breath feel your body becoming soft and more relaxed.

◆ Feel yourself becoming lighter and lighter until you begin to float upwards, high up into the air, until the houses and roads below are just tiny dots.

◆ Float still higher until you can see whole towns. Still higher, you rise until you can see whole countries, then continents and still higher you rise as you feel yourself floating off out into space.

◆ Watch the earth spinning and know that time is moving forward. Feel the years pass as you look down at the earth, yet you stay the same. In this space you are timeless. Focus on the earth and feel the decades pass, and finally know that 100 years has passed. Now look down at the earth, allowing your attention to be drawn to any place of interest.

◆ Are there any places you can see that have changed geographically – maybe floods, or land changes? What is happening with the environment? Are there any major changes with the weather? Scan the earth and see what you can see. Have there been any significant events? Scan the Middle East. Make a note of any impressions – allow two to three minutes after each question. Now do the same for China and Japan.

◆ Now look at America. Who is in power? Is the country prospering or struggling? Look at England. Do we still have a monarchy? If so, who is on the throne and are they popular? What is popular in sport? What do people do for entertainment? How has television developed and what is popular? What are we using for power and energy for heating our homes and powering our cars? How do people travel short and long distances? Have there been any medical breakthroughs? Anything else you feel is important?

◆ When you have seen enough, float back down into your current time and write down your findings. Know that you can visit this time whenever you wish to gain further knowledge.

◆ Carry out the Closing Down exercise (see page 44) to finish.

....

Before I discuss the results of this study in detail, I want to reveal my own predictions for the future and those revealed by clients in FLP sessions.

The Future Predictions

After each FLP session, I began to carefully write up my own findings about the 20, 50 and 100 year time frames, to build a complete profile. I also kept detailed records of predictions made by clients under various headings, for clarity. Where appropriate, I've transcribed parts of sessions with clients to add some extra detail. I've also grouped the information together into specific topics, listed below, and carefully selected information from each time frame. I hope you find this as exciting and fascinating as I do along with the people who helped me gather it, the pioneers of FLP who worked with me in my office in Bray.

Here are the areas we looked at:

◆ Environment

◆ Spirituality

◆ Government and military

◆ Education

◆ Medicine and health

◆ Finance

◆ Homes and home life

◆ Food

◆ Space travel

◆ Travel

Twenty Years in the Future

The Environment

I see many cities having a problem with pollution. The air looks almost thick and green, rather like the pea soupers of old, only this has a toxic edge to it. I can see people covering their mouths with scarves. This will affect parts of Europe, the United Kingdom, America, China and the Far East.

The exception will be Norway which will lead the way by having clean cities, with wonderful almost sweet clean air. It will be years ahead of other countries with cleaner efficient travel, and a major breakthrough with pollution.

There will be a new Nobel Prize for services to the planet. Norway will win.

Recycling becomes a huge political issue – there will be a lot less packaging and one company will become very successful and rich by producing biodegradable packaging that can be used to enrich the soil.

Many more people will grow their own fruit and vegetables,

especially those living in the countryside. Towns and cities will be too polluted.

Medicine and Health

The biggest breakthroughs are around health. Initially, drug companies and governments will try to push people away from natural remedies, but by 2027 they will embrace them and even provide evidence of their effectiveness. The evidence will be overwhelming.

Drug companies will stop trying to disprove natural remedies and highjack them instead! They will try to redeem themselves after strong evidence appears that some drugs taken today are in our water and cause health problems.

A cure for some types of cancer will be discovered. Treatment will be readily available but at an extremely high price. This will create all kinds of debates about healthcare, class and money.

Homeopathy will enjoy a resurgence, which will provide a quick cure for the skin and breathing problems prevalent at this time (including a new type of asthma that does not respond well to conventional drug therapy).

Cures for cerebral palsy and multiple sclerosis will be found. Both will be very simple, and I can see doctors almost kicking themselves for not having found them sooner.

Companies will be held much more accountable for the additives in their products. They will lose a number of high-profile court cases because they used additives with the full knowledge that they could have an adverse affect on health.

Finance

I can see a stock market crash in around 18 years' time. Be cautious, because the timing could be a bit out, but it will happen. This will badly affect America and Japan, resulting in mass unemployment and economic migration.

Home Life

More people will work from home and become more isolated. They will meet future partners through their own contacts such as family and friends. 'Stranger Dinner Parties,' will become popular as will meeting people through the internet.

Travel

Travel produces some of the most interesting developments, with very high-speed electric trains. They are clean, on time and (you will be pleased to hear) heavily subsidised. Many cities will adopt free travel. Services will not be like the cramped tube trains of today. Long-distance travel will be very cheap, but more like travelling first class on a plane. Governments will be forced to encourage people to leave their vehicles at home and will offer huge incentives.

Nuclear power will be widely used, but only as a transition phase until new power sources are pioneered.

I can see a super car, which I think has been developed by Ferrari. Most car companies will make little electric or hybrid smart cars. They will think small. The super car is clean, fast and beautiful. I hope I am not giving too much away about anything that they are working on right now; somehow this car manages to run on very little fuel. It appears to have two gears. I am not sure how this works; it may be semi automatic.

By comparison, other cars will be fumbling and inefficient. The electric and hybrid cars will be slow and run out of 'steam'. One car will run on gas, but I do not see this being very safe. There will be a lot of experiments with electric- and hydrogen-powered cars.

Expect in the coming years major problems with the quality of petrol and oil. Even in the next ten years, the quality of fuel will deteriorate resulting in more engine problems.

The flying car I mentioned in my first book *Instant Intuition* will be popular, especially in certain countries in the Middle East. Japan will be very keen, but with such a high population and the advent of a cheap mass produced version, there is chaos in the skies and on the ground.

Fifty Years in the Future

The Environment

As oil runs out in The Middle East, conflict fades and it will become a peaceful place. Many Middle Eastern countries will set themselves up as key business zones. They use their oil revenue wisely. I see them developing business/holiday centres as people will want to work in a beautiful environment and combine work and leisure more.

About one third of Africa will be uninhabitable because of searing heat. There will be 'no go' areas, with little in the way of government.

Government and Military

Many of my clients and myself have seen a short war between American and Japan. China will be involved and may even be the instigator. China will have a strong economy, having anticipated the future wisely.

Medicine and Health

People are much healthier with many illnesses either cured or contained. There are less genetic and birth defects, and doctors will be able to screen and treat babies whilst they are still in the womb.

Spinal injuries will be repaired. I see a kind of incredibly strong, but fine, thread used in operations; it looks like nylon. Such thread is already used in surgery – but this is a new thread developed specifically to treat spinal injuries.

Space Travel

America will lead a new space race with Russia and China close behind. The US will plan a mission to Mars, where they will find evidence of life.

There will be a space satellite monitoring Earth, looking beneath the surface. They will be able to monitor volcanic eruptions, earthquakes and mass movements of troops. They will also be able to detect weapons of mass destruction.

Scientists will find a way to communicate with beings from other worlds, after receiving a signal through space. It appears to be a series of bleeps almost like Morse Code. Quantum physicists will give up trying to show the governments that contact can be made by less primitive methods. They will develop a way to connect with beings from other times as well as other places.

Travel

Transport is so clean with high-speed electric trains. People will be less bothered about having their own personal vehicle as communal travel becomes much more efficient.

Flying around the world becomes easier, cleaner and quicker

as we fly just outside the earth's atmosphere. A trip to Australia can be done in little over two hours.

One Hundred Years in the Future

The Environment

The main environmental issue now is that the world is heating up, and this will continue for a long time. However, it will not be as big a problem as we see it, mainly because we will adapt and change as we always have done.

Parts of the Middle East will become uninhabitable and Africa will have new deserts; areas that are now very hot and dry will become barren. A number of new insects will appear in this environment and seem to thrive. People will at first be afraid of them but will find they are harmless and simply natural survivors.

The biggest problem to these countries will be water; and with an increasing world population, water will become more precious all over the globe. The trouble is some countries will have too much and others too little. This will be the major problem facing the planet in 100 years time, but scientists will be experimenting with weather control with some success, bringing much-needed water to many drought areas.

Carbon emissions do not seem to be an issue by then, though. Scientists have come up with a number of air cleaning solutions, and whilst not a quick fix, they will gradually clean the atmosphere. From what I can see, they will release particles into the air that seem to 'eat' any pollution.

In the coming years, we will continue to chop down our forests, but I can see that a century on they are protected in much the same way we protect certain endangered species of animals today.

England will have a monsoon season as it becomes wetter and hotter. Our winters will be milder and our summers longer and more humid. I would suggest to your grandchildren not to buy property in low-lying wet areas as they will become marshier over the decades.

World-wide, the seas and oceans will rise a few inches and create receding coastlines. Major cities and towns will gradually move back as new buildings are built. People will enjoy diving to see the old hotels, cafes, promenades, piers and fun fairs.

A great deal of the American coastline will recede and, unfortunately, New Orleans will cease to exist. I see a second New Orleans built a long way inland. It will not have the same 'vibe', however, and it will be called New New Orleans. Florida will also recede a long way. I feel that this will become one of the most flooded areas in America.

The water levels will have risen because the ice caps will almost have melted, but even in 100 years' time there will still be a small amount left at each cap.

There will be changes environmentally, it is inevitable, but overall I feel very optimistic about our future generations' ability to adapt and make the world a good clean safe place to live.

Spirituality

There will be many more religions, more splinter groups, and some will be based on spirituality and science – followers will believe that unless you can prove something then it's just fantasy.

Many people will turn to the Catholic faith because of its

strict schooling and strong guidelines. Catholics will have bigger families than they do in our current time, and the religion will enjoy resurgence.

Mainstream Islam will turn against fanatical factions. As a religion, followers will actively promote world wide peace.

The Jewish faith will become elitist and its mystical Scriptures will be well respected. Science will verify that many of the ancient teachings of the Kabbalah, a form of early mystic Judaism, contains information about things only just being discovered. Outsiders will want to join the Jewish faith — but will not be encouraged if they are not born into the faith or married into it.

An elite set of psychics will be used by the police and governments. There will also be a way to assess psychics and their abilities. It will become illegal to use their skills for industrial espionage, and if they step into banned areas they will be given the option to work for the government élite or house arrest. The designated homes for this have an energy field around them that inhibits their psychic ability.

By the way, government buildings and sensitive locations (such as military air bases, secret government sites and government buildings such as the Pentagon and the Houses of Parliament) will be protected by some sort of sonic wave. I believe this is already being developed, but it's causing problems to whales, dolphins and migrating birds.

Government and Military

I had images of what looked like an anti-aircraft guns, only much longer. They were aiming skyward at a 45-degree angle. At first it reminded me of old war movies and I thought I'd jumped back in time to the Second World War. Suddenly a beam of light shot out of the barrel and I realised that it was a laser. My impression was that it was a warning, rather than a machine designed to kill. What it was hitting out at I have no idea.

I observed a group of super soldiers. I could see that their concentration was superb. They noticed everything. They had super eyesight and hearing. At first I wondered if they were some sort of cyborg, but on closer examination I could see that they were human and their training and preparation was top notch. They are fed on super foods and specially grown and prepared nutrients. They are chosen by the age of eight, begin military training at 14, and undergo a huge screening programme. I also saw them being given implants that would warn them of danger.

Education

I was particularly interested in education and how we would bring up our children. I had a strong feeling that we could learn a great deal from the future to help our children become more highly evolved and intelligent.

I saw people carrying what looked like a stick, but with a flick of their wrist it rolled open revealing a tiny clip in which they inserted a microchip. These were the books of the future. Just imagine a scroll opening out to reveal a page – if you've ever tried to read a book on your computer screen you will know that it is a lot less pleasurable than having a book on your lap. This tool seemed to overcome this problem, yet incorporates future technology.

I noticed that people were also using the stick (I wish I knew the name of it) to watch television, to email, text and look at and speak to others. They were used by students to answer questions. The chip then assessed the question, answered it and told them what they needed to study further. Information links would then appear on the screen.

The stick was linked to a mini computer smaller than a mobile phone. This device would be useless to anyone other than the owner, as their own DNA activated it. This removed any worry about theft. I saw that there had been a spate of people snatching them whilst they were 'open', but the devices were modified to cut out as soon as this happened. There were very stiff penalties for touching someone's device. The sticks were personalised. People felt affection for them and gave them pet names.

I also saw children sitting in classrooms. They laughed as they were shown how people once used pen and paper. To them it was similar to us looking at cave people.

Apart from my own findings, I also sought the help of Sara Davidson, a freelance child and teenager education coach, who is developing new methods. She has trained with some of the most respected names in personal development, such as: Richard Bandler, Anthony Robbins, Paul McKenna and the Barefoot Doctor. She is a Master Practitioner of Neurolinguistic Programming and a member of the British Board of NLP (BBNLP). We both had our own reasons for researching future education, mine was to gain more information and insight into how the Trans people came about and progressed. For Sara, her reason was to be ten steps ahead of everyone else with techniques and ideas to make our children happier, more confident and more successful.

In her session, I took Sara forward 100 years and instructed her to closely examine how children are educated. Rapid eye movement began almost immediately as Sara hooked into the future. She told me, 'They use accelerated learning. Teaching is done using multi sensory experience; it's not just someone standing there and telling the students. If they're learning about cultures they will experience and feel what it was like to live at that time. They will even smell and taste the food people once ate.'

'How do they do this?' I asked.

'It's an advanced virtual reality programme as well using mock-up villages and towns and actual foods they have made.'

I was curious to know what at what age they began learning.

'From babies. Toddlers have constructive play. It is creative and educational.'

'How is teaching different from today?' I enquired.

'It is much more based on personal strengths and weaknesses – there is much more vocational training. They also teach human compassion, how to look after each other, and greater self-awareness. This is now a normal part of the teaching process. Children are also taught the impact of their actions,' Sara added. 'They are less selfish than kids of today.'

'It all sounds perfect. Are there any children with problems?' I prompted Sarah.

'Yes, but a lot less than today. If they are not academic a coach will find their strengths, such as sport or creativity, or recognising that they may make a great carer or actor, and the child is supported and directed into this area.'

You can find out more about Sara's work with her book *Girl Power: what you need to know but they don't teach you at school* on her website at www.teenagepower.com.

Medicine and Health

My first glimpse of a future hospital gave me a sense of peace. Although the walls were white, they had a soft hue to them and gentle music was playing in the background. I became aware of a sweet and gentle smell – it was not familiar to me, but again it made me feel calm. I realised that hospitals were deliberately using colours, smells and sounds to help people feel safe and comfortable. It worked.

My next impression was how few people were about. I could see that we needed a lot less medical help than we do today. I noticed that most individuals were being treated as outpatients, and so I assumed that they had minor ailments. However, I was stunned see that in fact some of them had very serious health problems, but the treatments were simple, fast-acting and non-invasive. The patients didn't need to be stuck in a hospital ward for weeks – a quick zap of a laser and they were off again.

In fact, time and time again I saw lasers being used in hospitals, so tell your grandchildren to invest in them! I saw a laser being shot through a crystal. This seemed to be an everyday treatment for many ailments. The lasers I saw were not like the equipment in use today. The laser ran through the semiprecious stone, or sometimes a diamond, which seemed to refine the effect. They could zap a tumour in no time. I also found in my one-to-one sessions with clients that many of them who are healers today will work in medicine in the future. Repeatedly, they mentioned using lasers with crystals. From what I saw, and what clients have told me, crystals and lasers will revolutionise medicine, as will medicines based on plant sources. Lasers will do everything from repair a wound or bone to eliminate tumours and fatty tissue.

There will be an antibiotic homeopathic remedy that is 100 times more effective than any antibiotic we have today, but it will have no ill effects.

I saw a hybrid plant that looked something like a cross between a cactus and an orchid. It was pink and purple. This plant had huge nutritional properties. A tiny sip of its sap each day would act as a tonic as well as an immune booster and high-dose vitamin shot.

The mind-body link will be widely accepted and using subliminal recording will be a normal part of aiding recovery.

Today we often try something and hope that it works, but it seems that the medicine of the future will have the guesswork taken out of it. Doctors of the future will be a little like the aeroplane pilots of today – computers do much of the work and most ailments will have a tried and tested cure.

There will also be much more emphasis on prevention and healthy living. I saw people discussing how we live today. They spoke with horror about our weak and polluted bodies. They saw us as almost unclean, full of toxins and eating diseased food. They laughed at what we called pure water.

Homes and Home Life

I took a peek at our future home life. I wanted to know if it would be very different from today, or if little had changed. If we are to believe the many sci-fi films, futuristic homes will be spartan and composed mainly of stainless steel. Everything will be controlled by machines and we will sit around in silver or white boiler suits and look quite androgynous. What I saw couldn't have been any further removed from this image.

I have often wondered why as we evolve we would make our homes more uncomfortable and not less? Luckily, the science fiction buffs have got it wrong.

The homes of the future will be extremely comfortable, and the good news is they're self-cleaning! Chairs and beds will automatically mould themselves to your shape and posture, and can be adapted to how hard or soft you want them to be.

Homes are a lot healthier – any paints, carpets and other home furnishings will be non-toxic and made from natural materials. Homes will be designed to keep us healthy, with separate space for exercise machines. This will be as essential as having a bathroom. Daily exercise at home will become the norm.

My overall impression was that life had become simpler. Many had opted for a more rural lifestyle, but even those still living in towns and cities had simplified their lives. There will still be plenty to do and plenty of choice, but people won't overload themselves with experiences as they do now. For example, sending an email whilst internet shopping – whilst also on hold on the phone. This kind of multitasking, which has become the norm for most of us, will become a thing of the past.

People seemed more at peace within themselves. Today, we are still quite childlike and want to experience and try so much *now*. But people of the future experience a great deal when they are young and curious through their education. Rather than simply reading or being told about things, kids in the future experience other cultures, countries, wars, etc, through a multi-sensory teaching tool. This means that when they are older, they have less need to try things, and are more choosy about what they are interested in. People settle into being more in touch with their inner selves and have a sense of contentment. They also seem to be far more connected to the people around them, especially their families.

Food

Our future selves will be foodies. Unlike the sci-fi films in which we are seen eating a pill or some gunk from something like a toothpaste tube for lunch, in actual fact we will love good food even more. Special chefs will be creating more and more unusual sensory gastronomical experiences. Eating these unusual foods will become the norm, and these super cooks will be seen as artists.

Space Travel

I was curious to know how far we'd progressed with space travel. I wondered if crafts of the future would be much different from those of today. They were not. I caught sight of a craft that was a long thin rocket pointing upwards – but the structure below had the appearance of a fairground ride, with sightseers waiting to board. This was a trip into space for fun.

There will be regular trips to the moon, mainly to collect resources such as minerals. At least one mineral, although unknown to us now, will be deemed very valuable. I also saw that there was a lot of secrecy around activities on the moon, with no one asking too many questions.

Travel

Our future selves will not travel great distances to work. Most will have jobs very near to where we live, using walkways or shuttle buses to get to the workplace. Many will work from home, being carefully monitored by bosses to check that work is being done.

To our future selves, travelling miles to a meeting or conference will seem ridiculous. Their technology will be so far advanced that colleagues and associates will appear to be in the same room.

Today we are seeing many new estates and towns being built where everything you need is nearby – and these estates are nice to look at too! There is usually one huge supermarket that will supply 90 per cent of your needs, a library and health centre within easy reach, plus a cinema and sports centre. This is how people will continue to live in the future and there will be emphasis on outdoor space too. In fact, all our needs will be catered for within a stone's throw of our homes. There will be no need to go to another area because it will be much the same as our current residence. For the same reasons, with loved ones living close by, families will tend not to move away or travel.

We (myself and other researchers) have found that these small towns of the future are strategically built on ley lines and with energy flows taken into account. Today our towns are made up of straight lines. The towns of the future will be more curved, almost like little tribal villages, with focal points in the centre and people living in curved streets surrounding a beautiful open space.

Most people will also own a small pod-like vehicle that can take off vertically. It will sit outside the home on a platform. I am not sure what fuels it, but it is non-polluting. I had the feeling that it was an electric car.

The Results of the Study - the World 100 Years On

Just to emphasise, there was some crossover with my original list of study topics (in my own personal sessions and those I began to record two years ago) in areas such as medicine, home life and travel. However, additional questions were added to widen the results and also for uniformity. The study covered various countries of the world to see how their society, economy and culture had developed. The environment and entertainment were touched on, too. The results, as you are about to find out, are fascinating.

The Middle East

A high percentage of the study's participants said that the Middle East would be far hotter and the population much lower. The heat was described as 'sickening, overwhelming and unbearable'. A great deal of the Middle East will be empty, but some high-tech cities will exist. People will have a very high standard of living there. These cities will be beautiful and peaceful.

There will no longer be any oil, and with the absence of oil will come an absence of conflict. The Middle East will be a peaceful, if mainly barren, place.

Some remote parts will be polluted by black and grey smog, although nowhere near cities or people, who will already have left these areas. The cause of the smog is not known.

China

At first it sounded as if the study's FLP travellers were describing two different countries, but then several people commented, 'It's as if China is split down the middle; one half is high tech the other very traditional.'

The findings either reflected one or the other, or both, depending on which part of China the participant was viewing.

The West side of the country seemed to be more traditional, with people wearing the same-coloured uniforms and travelling by bicycle. They seemed nervous and in a rush. Many people thought that there had been a war or an uprising. There was a water shortage and people lived in cramped conditions. There was little privacy.

The other side, the East, was very high tech. 'This is the first super city', was how one person described it. People travelled by a shuttle buses that ran through tubes. The standard of living was very high.

A number of people said that China needed to be watched, that the country was a threat and 'not to be trusted'. Other people described the Chinese government as 'slippery'. They would offer to trade 'but this would be a backhanded gesture'.

Japan

This was the most hi-tech country we saw. Japan led the way in technology of all sorts and the people had a very high standard of living. Several people commented how quiet it was even though there was a large population. Transport was again mainly through shuttle vehicles.

What Japan had gained in technology it had lost in the old ways. Traditions had faded, but people were healthy and led good lives.

A high percentage of people taking part in the study saw a huge earthquake that caused Japan to rebuild many of its cities. This was one of the reasons people that were happy. They appreciated what they had after a time of great loss.

The new cities had moving pavements and underground and underwater trains. The cities were hi-tech but beautiful, with trees and orange blossom. They used solar and wind power whenever possible, and cleanliness was of vital importance.

America

A number of people saw an Afro Caribbean American as president who was 'a fair and kind man'. Many participants said he had come to power after a corruption scandal that had changed the way the country handled politics. The scandal had led the way for change and had given the man the chance to run the country. With his guidance and vision, the USA was beginning to come out of a depression that had existed for 'a very long time'. They were about to invest in new technology and groundbreaking and pioneering science.

Many believed that America had been involved in a big war about 50 years previously.

America was no longer a super power; in fact it had little power by this time. Many people had gone back to a more rural, basic way of life and they seemed happier as a result.

Parts of the country were heavily polluted and unliveable. Many of the cities were tatty and squalid. Most people were poor, but the super rich had become even richer. The cities were very cramped and run down. Everyone agreed that the country was 'poor and no longer powerful'.

The UK
The Environment and Living

The United Kingdom was now small, with land mass being lost to the now higher sea levels. People described England as 'a different shape,' 'more round' and 'less of it'.

The climate had changed considerably, and most saw England with a tropical climate with warm evenings, lush countryside and strange new animals and plants.

Some cities had become almost no-go areas with tribal wars between groups from different backgrounds. People were confused about their nationalities, which had lead to conflict. The countryside was believed to be a much better place to live where village life seemed to thrive.

There were parts of the country that seemed to be trading in anything from currency to fish and commodities. The country wasn't poor, but it seemed more confused.

The Monarchy

Most participants felt that the UK still had a monarchy, but that they were rarely seen and carried little influence. A young girl was now queen but she seemed more like a May queen than a monarch. The position had a quaintness and was not taken very seriously, although the few other remaining royals seemed to be heavily guarded.

Sport

Over and over again, rugby was mentioned as a popular and key sport, with football still popular but trailing behind.

Huge stadiums were also mentioned, with massive crowds often watching hi-tech sports that seemed to combine physical ability with electronic equipment. This was like actually taking part in a computer game, similar to virtual reality. Other games used hi-tech gadgetry like electronic balls that travelled at great speeds.

There were never any disputes as to what had happened during a sporting event – every single movement was filmed, photographed and tracked by a floating camera that follows all the action so accuracy is guaranteed. The images come back via something like the cameras used in micro surgery today. Winning carried an even greater status than at present.

Entertainment

Most of my clients who took part in the study felt that families would spend more time together, and so family entertainment was highly popular and encouraged.

Television still existed, with thousands of channels and more interactive TV.

Although many people spent time with families, some people

had become more insular and spent their time alone and at home. Having so much entertainment made people less inclined to socialise. Apparently, this was one of the reasons so much emphasis was put on children learning social skills and interacting. There was a period of time when children attended school less often and this had led to socially inept people, with depression rising. This had now been turned around and people were mixing more.

There were many parks that were under a roof and so not under threat from the British weather!

Medicine and Health

As already highlighted by my own FLP sessions, there had been great advances in medicine and lower illness rates. Most cancers had been eradicated and Aids had been controlled.

From birth, people were health-profiled so that precautions could be taken. Surgery was less invasive but minor surgery would be conducted by robots, which ensured accuracy and cut down on infections because the robots were more sterile.

Natural remedies were taken more seriously and, coupled with better screening and profiling, many illnesses were nipped in the bud.

Whilst most illnesses we have today had been eradicated or become easily curable, there were some new health problems that medical science was trying to find cures for. These were mainly skin and lung diseases that had been caused by irritants in the environment and pollution.

How We Will Power Our Homes

The vast majority saw solar power being widely used. As one participant put it, 'It seems we make the most of global warming.' A great many people also saw homes having their own generator, although it was not clear how this was powered, and recycling water.

Throughout the study, it has been mentioned how many people go back to a more rural and natural way of living and this seems to hold true for how we power our homes. The rural population used up many fewer resources.

There was a natural fuel, something grown, renewable and used en mass that effectively created a lot of energy from minimal materials. It also had incredibly low CO_2 emissions. Wind power was also popular, but overall solar power ruled.

Travel

In this section of the study, we gained a fascinating insight into how we will live. Vast cities with walkways between buildings were described, and small shuttles running through tubes travelling at great speeds. These were highly fuel efficient and non-polluting. In fact, there was no pollution from most travel and only a slight problem caused by air travel. It seemed the world would wake up and smell the coffee – or at least the toxins in the air.

Several people described shuttles like 'a roller coaster zooming about at high speed, twisting and turning' getting people from A to B in no time at all.

Air craft travelled much faster, with some leaving the earth's atmosphere and returning in at least a tenth of the time they do today.

Bicycles had become more popular as people became more health and pollution conscious.

Free-flow Questions

The last part of the study included the question, 'Is there anything significant you wish to mention from you guided FLP session?'

A number of people mentioned again that they thought there would be a war in about 50 years' time. This seemed to involve America and Japan, although not necessarily just those two or against each other.

The Far East becomes much more powerful.

Many people mentioned a disease affecting the skin and lungs.

How to Find the Evolved Future You

This exercise works best in a darkened room and if you sink into a comfy chair.

◆ Close your eyes. Relax and leave behind all that has happened to you today.

◆ Carry out the Opening Up technique, as outlined on page 42, to begin.

◆ Clear your mind of your thoughts and feelings and feel yourself floating and relaxing. And as you sink into the chair, imagine that the chair is floating through time and space. Feel that you are floating away from your current life beyond your current time and place.

◆ Feel the chair arrive and land on a platform and as you do so, you realise that there is nothing around you. You are suspended in time and space. You have stepped outside your current reality, and from here you can view anything that you want to.

◆ Clear your mind and know that you are about to view yourself in 100 years' time. You will view and connect with yourself whatever form you take at that time. Feel the information floating towards you and know that in front of you will be the future you – the you in 100 years.

◆ Allow this to come into view. Whoever and whatever you are in the future you will be made of energy, just as you are now. Connect with the energy that is the future you.

◆ Where are you? Are you on Earth or somewhere else? Are you a Trans Person? Or a Grunter? Maybe you are a Light Being. What does this feel like? Know that you can communicate telepathically with the future you. In your mind, ask the future you what your soul purpose is.

◆ Now ask what you need to do right now in your current time, and what advice you have for yourself. Remember, the future you is highly evolved and full of wisdom. We all wish we had hindsight, and now you can have the benefit of this.

◆ Ask what you need to know.

◆ Now step into the future you. How does this feel? Connect with the highly evolved you. Become one with the future you.

◆ Absorb the wisdom, the contentment and the higher energy of the future you. Take what you need from the future you and allow any thoughts, feelings and energy to flow into your solar plexus. As you do so, put one hand on your solar plexus as if you are locking in the energy.

◆ Now float out of the future you but keep the wonderful, highly evolved energy with you and bring it with you back to your present time.

◆ Any time you want to connect with this energy, simply put one hand on your solar plexus and the energy of the future you will be with you.

◆ Don't forget to carry out the Closing Down technique, as outlined on page 44, to finish.

The following exercise, The World, will link you to everyday life 100 years from now, giving you a taste of how we will live and feel. By tapping into the future this way you will see what has improved and connect with a better way of living and being. This technique will also give you confidence that the world will still exist, and will be an even better place. This knowledge will take away any worries or fears that doom mongers so like to encourage.

I love this exercise because practising it has reassured me that the world will be a good place for my great grand children and the children of the world and beyond.

The World

◆ Carry out the Opening Up technique, as outlined on page 42, to begin.

◆ Imagine you are looking down on the world. Become aware of just how long the world has been here – ever-changing, ever-evolving. People, creatures and plants have come and gone and the world still exists. The world has been hotter and it has been colder. The lands have changed shape and so have the seas, oceans and mountains, but still the world is here.

◆ Feel a sense of peace as you look down on the world.

◆ And now as you look down on the world know you are looking at in exactly on hundred year's time. How does it feel? It is more peaceful than it is today? Does it feel different in any way? Are there more or fewer people?

◆ Now look down at your own current country and imagine you are floating all the way down in that very place and arriving there at exactly 100 years from your present time. Look around you and see how people live their everyday lives at this time. How do they travel? What are there homes like? What work do they do? Are they happy? What are their concerns?

◆ Imagine you are one of them. What will you have for dinner? Where will you sleep? What work do you do? What will you do in your leisure time? Who do you mix with? What are your beliefs? What is important to you?

◆ Run through an average day and experience life in one 100 years' time.

   Ask yourself what you can learn from this? How can this experience benefit you right now?

◆ When you are ready, float back to where you were before.

View the world and know that you have tasted a little bit of the future.

◆ Carry out the Closing Down technique, as outlined on page 44, to finish.

....

The World Study began as a little curiosity to see if others would come up with the same images as myself. By the time the questionnaires came back, I knew that we were gaining valuable information that we can use right now to make the world a better place. I do realise that as humans we have not got things drastically wrong and although we still have much to learn, and need to lose some of our more primitive and selfish ways, we're not a bad lot at all. And we become more kind, clever and aware as time goes on.

Interestingly, the participants of the study told me that they slept better at night or had a new sense of peace after viewing the world. Everyday worries about climate change, wars and the environment faded as they what we can to make improvements and clean up any problems we have created. They added that this didn't make them complacent – if anything, they became more aware and keen to help bring the good changes forward in time by joining an environmental group, recycling or using public transport. It has been good for me to know that Future Life Progression has spurred people into action.

EPILOGUE
Watch this Space

When I first came across Future Life Progression I had no idea how far it would take me, and even now I'm still learning about the future every day. Sometimes the information comes through my own visions, often whilst working with my clients or groups. Yet I know that this is only the beginning – knowledge comes to us when we are ready, and discoveries are made when the time is right.

As you worked your way through *The Future Is Yours*, and the book's exercises, you will have discovered that time is not what you think it is – or have been led to believe. You will have learnt how to make time elastic, how to change and stretch it, rather than be the victim of it.

You have now seen how Future Life Progression can aid you in your personal life, helping you mend a broken heart by taking you forward and seeing your new love. You will have also read the story about the lady who was able to see that she will be reunited in her next lifetime with her beloved husband who had passed away. Other case studies in the book have revealed how people have seen themselves with a new partner, then gone on to meet and marry them. It is easy to get stuck in a romantic rut, but Future Life Progression can help you to find happiness in love.

You will have looked at how Future Life Progression can help you in your working life by finding your true vocation, or the right business. I have also shown you how to avoid bad moves that could potentially ruin you. The process can even show you how to choose the right business partner, so if you run your own business and are looking to expand, this technique could come in handy. I hope truly that you find success and happiness in your vocation like hundreds of my clients. Don't be afraid to make changes.

In the chapter on trends and investment, I touched on Future Life Progression and playing the stock market, and how this process can give you the edge in areas that can be minefields. You will have gained insight into finding the next big thing in property or the next up-and-coming property hotspot. Thanks to the techniques you have learnt, you will be able to make better decisions about where, and where not, to live.

If you need to discover the next trends in industry, fashion and much more, and what fields will thrive and which will falter, you have the techniques. You can even tap into your own future genius to find the novel, play, painting or song, or perhaps an invention, an idea or a new way of working that will save the world money or resources. You have an inner genius, and you can use Future Life Progression to connect to it.

You may have discovered the deep-rooted cause of problems that have plagued you on this soul journey, and probably in past lives. But now you have been given the tools to break these bonds and clear the patterns. Future Life Progression has helped many people rid themselves of a pattern of abuse by taking them to a time when they are happy, in love and confident – even if this is not until their next incarnation. The good news is that I have shown you how to bring the good elements of the future right back into your present time. You do not want to wait for better times – you need them right now.

You will have looked at yourself as a soul, as someone who has been here before and will be here again. Your soul has spanned centuries, and many lives, and you have dipped into your past, present and future in order to gain awareness of patterns, of your soul's purpose and how you can find and stay on your path. You have learnt to use the technique of finding the positive aspects of your future and connecting these aspects to you and bringing them into your present time. After all, who wants to wait ten years for that perfect partner or lucky break?

You will have met the future, more highly evolved, you, and gained the benefit of hindsight. You will have found your own future wisdom and have had a taste of a more positive world that is to come, where the human race finally grows up and works together instead of against each other.

I have also revealed how myself, and others, have used Future Life Progression to view world events. We have seen how the world will be not just in the next few years, but way into the future.

It feels like a million years ago that my soldier friends and I saw snippets of the events of 11 September 2001. At the time we were mystified, and also distraught because it was upsetting to think we'd seen something so tragic yet had not been able to stop or change the events. Then when the terrorist attack happened we wondered why we had seen something if we couldn't change it. Now I know that with your help we will be able to build a profile of future events. Some of you may have an image, others a strong thought or feeling, but between us all we can build a profile and may be able to warn others – or even change the events to something of a more positive nature.

Where Do we Go From Here?

Do keep practising the exercises, even if it is just for ten minutes several times a week. There is not an ideal number of times per week as everyone is different, but with regular practice that suits you, you will become more and more proficient. You will get sharper and better information as time goes on. Initially, you may be drawn to a particular topic such as love, or work, and you will find exercises such as The Gallery (page 52) or The Doors (page 85) to suit your most important needs. Then, as you work your way through the book you will discover that some exercises suit you more than others. Eventually, you will find one that allows you to take little trips to the time zone and topic that you most need to know about. This will become your own special exercise that you use the most.

I regularly use The Doors to make business decisions and The Lift to see how far I am progressing – to see if there is any information that is of use to me now. Other times I use The Karmic Sandwich to clear any negative patterns I have become aware of. You will find your own best exercises, and over time they may change as your needs change.

You can get involved too and take part in the study in this book (The World in 100 Years, on page 231) which you can also download free as a guided visualisation from my website www.futurelifeprogression.com. Between us we can build a profile of what will happen in the world, and to the human race as a whole. We can use this information to gain a sneak preview of developments in medicine, travel and energy sources.

You can also log on and read the Future Life Progression experiences of others – and add your own. I cannot wait to hear your discoveries, so please do visit and drop me an email.

We will be adding more guided visualisations to the website so that you can experience the whole range of exercises. With your help, we can compile information that will help us all, not just this lifetime but in our future lifetimes and in our soul's journey as well.

If investments work for you, then I ask that you give a portion to charity. My favourites are Help the Aged because older people's blood, sweat and tears have brought us this far in life, and Save the Children, because children are our future. The greatest investment we can make is to invest in our future, in our children and the children of the world. As we become more aware that there is more to life than we had realised, we see ourselves as a soul, as a being of energy, and not just the flesh and bones of our bodies.

The human race is going through a time of change. As you look around you will see people becoming more spiritually aware. I believe that we are evolving very quickly and we are now ready to look into our future and the future of the world.

Recently someone said to me, 'But if we use Future Life Progression to progress in life it means we won't have to struggle and go through hell in order to learn. Shouldn't we suffer to grow?'

In short, no! I truly believe that we can learn quickly, and we do not need to have traumatic, long-term relationships in order to grow – we can find out after a fortnight if someone is wrong for us. We do not need to be in jobs in which we are not appreciated and do not shine. Instead we can move forward and find out where we will be brilliant and be of service. What can we possibly learn from being held back?

You can learn and grow without suffering. You have grown enough to be able to connect with your future self and be told that you have got it wrong, that you must change direction or that you are being selfish and need to change your ways. You are big enough to receive this information because you are ready. Otherwise you would not have been drawn to Future Life Progression.

I have looked at our futures many times, and it has made me very optimistic about our future and the future of the human race. We are about to grow up. The world will become a better place where we work together more and see our similarities, not our differences. We will have the right priorities, and we will value ourselves.

In *The Future is Yours* you have learnt to move through time to glimpse your past and, more importantly, your future. I hope your journeys into the future bring you much happiness in your present lifetime.

Watch this space – our journey is just beginning.

CONTACTING THE AUTHOR

To contact Anne Jirsch, please email anne@futurelifeprogression.com

or visit her website at

www.futurelifeprogression.com where you can download the guided visualisation on The World in 100 Years, and share your FLP experiences.

Bibliography

Bruce, A., *Beyond the Bleep*, The Disinformation Company, 2005

Buchanan, L., *The Seventh Sense, Pocket Books*, 2003

Goldberg, B., *Time Travellers from Our Future*, Book World/Blue Star, 1999

Gribbin J., Gribbin M., *A Life In Science*, Penguin Group, 1997

Monroe, R., *Ultimate Journey*, Bantam Doubleday Dell Publishing Group, 1996

Radin, D., *Entangled Minds*, Pocket Books, 2006

Snow, C. S., *Mass Dreams of the Future*, McGraw-hill Publishing Company, 1989

Talbot, M., *The Holographic Universe*, Harper Collins Publishers, 1991

Targ, R., and Puthoff, H., *Information and uncertainty in remote perception research*, Journal of Scientific Exploration, vol 17, no.2, 2003

White, R., *Working With Your Soul*, Piatkus Books, 2007

Wolfe, F. A., *The Yoga of Time Travel*, Quest Books, 2004

Zukav, G., *The Seat of the Soul*, Random House Ltd, 1990

Index